CONTENTS

T0335167

INTRODUCTION

BY DAVID L. BRISTOW, EDITOR

This is a special publication of *Nebraska History*, separate from our numbered series of issues that we've published for more than a hundred years. Here we present an anthology of past articles about the women's suffrage movement in Nebraska, along with some new content and illustrations.

August 2, 2019, marks the centennial of Nebraska's ratification of the Nineteenth Amendment to the US Constitution. Nebraska was the fourteenth state to ratify. A year later, on August 18, 1920, Tennessee's ratification gave the amendment the approval of three-fourths of the states as the Constitution requires. It then became the law of the land.

The Nineteenth Amendment states that a citizen's right to vote "shall not be abridged or denied... on account of sex." It's often said that the amendment guarantees all American women the right to vote, but laws *guarantee* nothing. Even the Constitution can be ignored if the public allows it. Even as the Nineteenth Amendment was debated, Southern states had already used intimidation and discriminatory laws to deny African American men their Fifteenth Amendment voting rights. This unconstitutional robbery was now extended to African American women voters. This happened with the acquiescence of the nation as a whole.

By 1919 Nebraska no longer challenged the voting rights of citizens of color, but not all Nebraska-born people were citizens. In a famous court case originating in Omaha, the US Supreme Court ruled in *Elk v. Wilkins* (1884) that a reservation-born Winnebago man was not a citizen because he owed allegiance to his tribe—despite the man's renunciation of such allegiance. Over the years many Native Americans gained citizenship through military service or by accepting individual land allotments under the Dawes Act, but many others were excluded until the Indian Citizenship Act of 1924.

The Nineteenth Amendment, in other words, is part of a larger national conversation about voting rights and equal representation—a conversation that pre-dates the Constitution and continues to this day. With that in mind, read these articles while asking big questions:

How did people expect the country to change if women got the vote? How did they think the vote might change women? What gains did people hope for, and what losses did they fear? Why did some strong, active women oppose suffrage? How did matters of class, religion, race, and national origin influence the discussion? What alliances were formed, and what outside agendas shaped those alliances? The answers can be surprising.

Turn the page to read Ann Wiegman Wilhite's overview of the suffrage movement in Nebraska; the articles by Bloomberg, Hickman, and Potter each develop a portion of that story in more detail. Two short pieces tell of Nebraska incidents involving two nationally famous suffragists (Susan B. Anthony and Carry A. Nation), while new articles describe two Nebraska-born suffragists (Doris Stevens and Rheta Childe Dorr) who achieved national prominence.

Nebraska suffrage-related artifacts are featured in a photo section near the end of the book. Finally, a "Primary Sources" appendix lists women's suffrage resources at History Nebraska—resources that we hope will inspire school papers, National History Day projects, academic theses and dissertations, and future articles for Nebraska History.

Below: Young Nebraskan woman prepares for suffrage parade in Blair, 1914. RG1073-2

Paper Poster: Printed and mounted to rod and ribbon for display. 4622-12

Yellow Ribbon; a select palette of colors were used to show solidarity; yellow was a prominent choice. 4610-34

WOMAN SUFFRA
DEBATE
UDITORIUM
5 P. M.

Votes for Women

Sixty-Five Yrs, Till Victory

A History of Woman Suffrage in Nebraska

by Ann L. Wiegman Wilhite

Sixty-Five Years Till Victory:
A History of Woman Suffrage in Nebraska
by Ann L. Wiegman Wilhite

Men. Everywhere. Sitting on benches, standing between the seated, leaning against the walls. Hardly able to make her way through the crowd, the small, auburn-haired young lady took her place on the speaker's platform. She spoke simply, yet eloquently. After an hour and a half of attentive silence, the audience broke into great applause.

Who was this courageous, eloquent woman with the prim bonnet, simple black dress and matching pantalet? Only six months before—on July 4, 1855—she had stood in front of the Douglas House and addressed curious Omahans. Impressed, some of those listeners—anxious to promote Nebraska's image as a progressive state— had invited her to give a similar speech here, before the Territorial Legislature. Thus, less than eight years after the first woman's rights convention, the Nebraska Legislature heard their first speech on woman's rights. What did the women want? Emphatically, Amelia Bloomer replied:

"We claim all the rights guaranteed by the Constitution of the United States to the citizens of the Republic. We claim to be one-half the people of the United States, and we deny the right of the other half to disfranchise us."[1]

According to the *Council Bluffs Chronotype*, Mrs. Bloomer's arguments "had met with much favor."

"We may doubt the policy for women to vote; but who can draw the line and say that naturally she has not a right to do so? Mrs. Bloomer, though a little body, is among the great women of the United States; and her keen intellectual eye seems to flash fire from a fountain that will consume the stubble of old theories until woman is placed in her true position in the enjoyment of equal rights and privileges. Her only danger is in asking too much."[2]

The House did not think Mrs. Bloomer was asking too much: they responded to her arguments by passing a suffrage bill (fourteen to eleven) on January 25, 1856. The Council (upper house), however, was bickering over county boundaries. The session, limited to forty days, adjourned sine die before they could take a vote.

"I was assured by Gov. Richardson and others," wrote Mrs. Bloomer in her journal, "that the bill would undoubtedly have passed had a little more time been allowed them."[3] Had it passed, Nebraskans would have been the first in America—and in the world—to enfranchise women.[4] The forward-looking legislators who favored equal rights went unrewarded, with the exception of their eloquent leader, General William Larimer. The suffrage opponents gave Larimer a petticoat "over which there came near being a general melee."[5]

Thus, Nebraska Territory maintained the male securely on his throne. Statehood promised no immediate change, for the 1866 constitution explicitly limited both electoral eligibility (Article II, Section 2) and constitutional incumbency (Article III, Section 4) to men.

Proponents of the woman's rights movement, however, did not consider the printed word infallible, especially when it denied women the franchise. With the assistance of Mrs. Elizabeth Cady Stanton, Miss Susan B. Anthony and George Francis Train, they inaugurated their suffrage campaign in Omaha on November 15, 1867. The same year the Legislature passed the following statute, which became effective in 1869:

"*Every inhabitant* at the age of 21 years, residing in the district, and liable to pay a school-district tax therein, shall be entitled to vote at any district meeting." (Italics added.)

Women now had school suffrage, a step forward that Nebraska was the second state to make. But she could not stay ahead. In 1875 the Legislature changed the wording of the law to "every male citizen and unmarried woman;" it would take another six years to again include married women.[6]

In 1871 came the Constitutional Convention, where woman suffrage was repeatedly discussed. At first the suffragists' wishes were treated with a mock

---

Opposite Page: Amelia Bloomer (1818-1894) lived much of her adult life in Council Bluffs, Iowa. She tried to convince the Nebraska Territorial Legislature to adopt women's suffrage in 1856. Artwork based on engraving from *History of Woman Suffrage*, Volume I, 1887.

solemnity. Mr. B. I. Hinman, for instance, presented the following resolution on June 24:

> WHEREAS; it is charged by woman (suffragists) that drunkenness, debauchery, fraud, and all grades of vice and villany [sic], are the rule of the day owing to the corruption of the male sex...
>
> RESOLVED. That the elective franchise shall be conferred on females alone.
>
> 2nd. That the word "male" shall be stricken from the Constitution wherever the same occurs, and the word "female" substituted there for... [the rest of the resolution proposed that all the traditional male occupations and duties be given to women].[7]

By August, however, much serious attention was given to the question. Mr. E. Estabrook was the first to speak at length in favor of enfranchising women, quoting from Madison, Paine, Jefferson, Blackstone and others for support. How could one say that politics would desex women? What of Queen Victoria? "Why, sir, Queen Victoria is not only at the head of the government, but if there is a mother that comes up to the full standard of perfect motherhood, if there is one it is Queen Victoria herself."[8] In response to the clause that would give the vote to all males except infants, the insane or criminals, he asked: what of woman's exclusion?

THE BLOOMER COSTUME.

"...is she imbecile, is she a lunatic, is she idiotic, is her intellect immature? No, but she is a woman; and not a man.... I have been told, Mr. President, that it was not the intention at the time of the creation of this earth that woman should belong to the governing power. I want to know, Mr. President, how you found that out?"[9]

The opposition responded with eloquent, prosaic orations eulogizing all that is noblest and purest of womanhood. To expose the delicate, sensitive, refined woman to the vices of politics would be unthinkable. One argument claimed that giving woman the vote would destroy the divinely ordained institution of marriage, sowing seeds of dissention between husband and wife. "A house divided against itself can not stand." This elevated discourse concluded:

"Finally, Mr. President, I really think that if the ballot was placed in the hands of women, the old American eagle, that stands with one foot upon the Alleganies [sic] and the other upon the Rocky mountains, whetting his beak upon the ice-capped mountains of Alaska, and covering half the southern gulf with his tail, will cease to scream and sink into the pits of blackness, of darkness concentrated, where the shrieks of lost spirits will forever echo and reecho through cavernous depths unknown and be no more forever."[10]

Though numerous resolutions were considered, the convention was unable to reach a solution; the issue was conveniently shifted onto the people via the separate submission device. But the people accepted neither the proposal (12,495 to 3,502) nor the constitution (8,627 to 7,986).

"The women of America,.." wrote Walt Whitman in his *Democratic Vistas* of 1871, are "great... as man, in all departments; or rather, capable of being so, soon as they realize it, and can bring themselves to give up toys and fictions, and launch forth, as men do, amid real, independent, stormy life." The women of Nebraska (specifically of Hebron in Thayer County) seemed to accept this challenge after the 1871 defeat, and the next decade saw a spurt of suffrage activity.

Another constitution was drafted in 1875, based largely upon the 1871 constitution. The suffrage issue no doubt had received much attention again at the constituting convention, but records of the proceedings do not exist. Nevertheless, any franchise efforts were unsuccessful. The accepted constitution (30,332 to 5,474) of 1875 denied suffrage to the mentally ill, to criminals—and to women.

In 1876 The *Hebron Journal*, published by Erasmus M. Correll, became the first paper to discuss equal rights. Three years later, it devoted an entire column to the political interests of women with Mrs. Lucy Correll in charge. In November of 1878, Susan B. Anthony won many converts in Hebron with her lecture, "Bread vs. the Ballot."

Another leading suffragist, Mrs. Elizabeth Cady Stanton, came to Hebron in April of 1879 and organized the first Woman's Suffrage Association in Nebraska. The Thayer Association grew from fifteen to seventy-five members and eventually included many leading businessmen.[11] Seeing the advantages of organization and unity, the suffragists formed a state association in January of 1881 with Harriet S. Brooks as the first president. A few months later the *Western Woman's Journal* was established to give the association a voice. Headed by Mr. Correll, this pioneer suffrage paper, 'sparkling as the dewdrops,"[12] appeared monthly in active support of woman's equality.

What happened at a typical suffrage meeting? The agenda of a Gage County meeting consisted of reviewing the suffrage movement in England, reading a sketch of 'Mrs. Oliver's Church" and quoting from articles by Julia Ward Howe. It concluded with two musical selections: 'Come Where the Lillies Bloom" and "The Land of the Swallows."[13]

American Woman and Her Political Peers.

COPYRIGHT, 1893, BY HENRIETTA BRIGGS-WALL.

Opposite Center: Bloomer's name is associated with a style of clothing she promoted (but did not invent). The "Bloomer costume," shown here in an 1851 Currier and Ives lithograph, featured loose-fitting trousers under a short skirt. Library of Congress

Above: "American Woman and Her Political Peers" by Henrietta Briggs-Wall (1893). The picture features suffragist and Woman's Christian Temperance Union president Frances E. Willard surrounded by the faces of an "idiot," convict, Indian, and witch. Suffragists sometimes used nativist and racist appeals to protest their political exclusion. HN 12921-1b

The enthusiasm of the suffrage associations soon stirred up support for another amendment. Submitted to the Legislature in 1881, it met the opposition of two principal groups: the "wets," who felt woman suffrage meant prohibition, and a large middle group who felt women belonged at home. Nevertheless, by a vote of fifty-one to twenty-two (eleven absent) in the House and twenty-two to eight in the Senate, a joint resolution was accepted to submit an amendment to the people. The ease with which it passed, however, was misleading; as A. E. Sheldon indicates in *Nebraska, the Land and the People* (I, 594), many legislators voted just to get rid of the suffrage question and to pass the buck to the voters.

The suffragists were encouraged by their proposal's acceptance and worked zealously behind the scenes: organizing associations, raising money, securing press outlets, distributing material and corresponding.

The Hon. Mr. Correll, who had supported the successful bill in the Legislature, was rewarded for his efforts by Mrs. Lucy Stone. In the fall of 1881, he received the presidency of the American Woman's Suffrage Association. Nebraska's leadership was nationally recognized; the acceptance of the 1882 amendment assumed new importance.

Nebraska Land
(Air: "Annie Laurie")

Oh, Nebraskaland, Nebraska,
    Our state so good and true,
We'll give the equal franchise
    To men and women, too;
To all the women, too,
    And their votes none can decry,
And for women's rights and suffrage,
    We will lay us down and die,
Oh, Nebraskaland, Nebraska
    Will not long the right refuse,
But grant to every woman
    Her just and lawful dues:
Her just and lawful dues,
    And their votes none can decry,

And for women's rights and suffrage,
    We will lay us down and die.

The culmination of this feverish activity came with the election year, 1882. The autumn campaign opened with meetings in the Boyd Opera House in Omaha on September 26-28. The accounts of these meetings in the September 27 *Omaha Republican* (p. 8) were encouraging:

"Considered as a series of political meetings the suffrage convention had more hearers than all the democratic meetings and conventions held in Omaha during the last 5 years. The audiences were truly representative, embracing the business, professional and working interests of our city, and composed very largely of voters and citizens influential in politics."

Nebraska women were aided not only by the press (the majority of newspapers declared for suffrage), but also by the most talented suffragists in the country. To one hundred Nebraska towns came Mrs. Stone (Blackwell) and her husband, Miss Anthony, Miss Phoebe Couzins, Mrs. Stanton and several others, including Mrs. Clara Newman, a German who spoke with the German people. "The woman suffragists are here in force and talent," wrote one reporter, "and they will succeed in giving truth a tongue. Woman suffrage will be a law in Nebraska."[14]

What were the basic arguments of the suffrage supporters? Summarized from the Woman Suffrage Platform of 1882,[15] they were:

1) suffrage is women's birthright as citizens of the United States;

2) equal suffrage is inherent to democratic—republican philosophy and to the meaning of the Declaration of Independence and the Constitution;

3) the larger electorate would eventually increase the strength and power of the country; and

4) women share the concern and consequences in governmental affairs, and thus should also be able to share power in controlling that government; they cannot accept taxation without representation.

On hearing these arguments, a fair, thoughtful man should have seen their logic. But opponents refused to

Below Top: Suffrage parade, circa 1914. The women's parasols are labeled with the names of selected states and the years they granted the vote to women. A banner proclaims "Nebraska Next." From the collections of the Nebraska Woman Suffrage Association. HN RG1073-7

Below Bottom: Before a women's suffrage parade in Blair, July 11, 1914. HN RG1073-4

listen. The *Omaha Herald* classed woman suffrage as a "species of lunacy." Other editorials in the *Herald* (typical of the opposition) gave such convincing arguments against suffrage as "no woman has ever had the courage to confess to wrinkles." Or: "A woman in Denver got so mad that she bursted a blood vessel and died on the instant. But women when they get mad invariably burst something."[16]

How many people accepted these arguments is, of course, unknown. More common were those that feared for the future of the home and motherhood.

"Should a woman neglect her home to join in the giddy turmoil of the world, either the propagation of the race would ultimately cease, or the mortality of children, which is now so great, owing to the relegation of the tender offsprings to artificial nourishment, as to alarm the most thoughtful people, would multiply infinitely."[17]

But however they argued, on November 7 the voters rejected the amendment by a margin of two to one. Despite the eloquence, support, logic and optimism of the suffragists, "they were not able to prevail against the inherent prematurity of their issue."[18] Nebraska had again lost the opportunity to boost her image: acceptance of this amendment would have made Nebraska the first state in the Union to give women the right to vote.

How did the suffragists accept defeat? Some thought further attempts were futile and turned their interests elsewhere, as did the Grand Island Suffrage Society which donated its funds for the building of a library.[19] Others saw "no cause for discouragement but great need of continued and renewed activity."[20] They were determined to fight, regardless of the opposition. As one suffragette said to a weaker sister, "Call on God, my dear. She will help you."

Activity resumed in January of 1887 with the arrival of Susan B. Anthony to address the state suffrage convention in Lincoln. Since full suffrage seemed to be temporarily unattainable, interest turned to municipal suffrage. A Senate bill received favorable committee action, but, though conservative in its demands, was not voted upon. "Man was afraid of petticoat government. He had been king so long that he did not wish to make room for a queen."[21] Attempts were made again in 1889, 1891,

1893, 1897 and 1909, but each municipal suffrage bill met defeat.

On January 20, 1909, Senate File 120 was introduced to amend Article VII, Section I of the constitution. It passed the House sixty-two to thirty-four and the Senate eighteen to thirteen, lacking two votes of the necessary three-fifths majority. A second vote was taken in the Senate eleven days later, but the suffrage proposal failed again. "It is generally believed the bill of 1909 was defeated by the liquor interests," wrote Mrs. Grace Mason Wheeler to a suffragist friend in New York.[22]

A famous British suffragette, Mrs. Emmaline Pankhurst, came to Omaha in 1911 and "took this town by storm."[23] Two years later, another suffrage amendment was introduced in the House, but it too failed in a close vote: forty-nine to fifty with one person absent. Senators explained their negative votes:

"[enfranchising women would] double the expense of election with practically the same result and if not a division in the family.... the introduction of women into the man's political world of strife and contention, of ambition, jealousies, and bitterness as we know it to be, would tend directly to the decay of the home.... even under woman suffrage no woman would ever sit in the White House as President, for the reason that not one could be found who would admit she was 35 years of age...."[24]

Senator Charles H. Busch remarked that this state had adopted (in 1912) the initiative and referendum to meet such problems. The suffragists took the hint and circulated petitions in every county during the spring and summer of 1913. The names totaled 48,035 and made at that time, according to a Lincoln paper, "the largest [initiative petition] that has ever been filed in Nebraska."[25]

> Nebraska! Nebraska!
>   She's all right,
>   Organize! Organize! and in the fight!
>   Right up the stream we'll row our boat,
>   For Nebraska women are bound to vote.

And bound they were! Nebraska women made the 1914 campaign the most enthusiastic to date, employing everything from songs, slogans and street meetings to parades and posters. This time they were assured of victory.

Let the Lassies Try
(Air: "Coming through the Rye")

If a lassie wants the ballot
    To help to run the town,
If a lassie gets the ballot,
    Need a laddie frown?
Many a laddie has the ballot
    Not so bright as I,
Many a laddie votes his ballot
    Overcome with RYE.

CHORUS
Every laddie has the franchise
    Nane, They say, hae I
Hands and hearts and brains for service
    Let the lassie try.

If a lassie works for wages
    Toiling all the day,
When her work the laddie's equals
    Give her equal pay.
If a body pays the taxes
    Surely you'll agree
That a body earns the franchise
    Whether HE or SHE

But they did not agree. The election returns showed 90,738 for the amendment, but 100,842 against. Why did the amendment fail? Two strong reasons appear: (1) the possibility of fraudulent voting and (2) the activities of the opposition.

First, was there fraud? After the election Attorney General Willis E. Reed stated "that most of the amendments ... would have carried if pains had been taken to correctly count the vote."[26] Fraudulent counting had been reported, but a recount bill was not offered in the Legislature. Too many feared their interests would be hurt.

The other reason for the suffrage defeat was strong opposition from three principal groups. The first was comprised of leading business' and professional men, such as those in Omaha who signed the "Omaha Manifesto" against suffrage. The second group consisted of women who did not want the vote. Some were strictly *Hausfrau* who wanted only *Kuche, Kinder* und *Kirche*; others were working women who felt they benefited more from men's efforts on their behalf than by equal suffrage.[27]

It was, however, the third group that played the most important role. These were the foreign-born citizens, specifically those influenced by the German-American Alliance. Having brewery interests, the Alliance was strongly against woman suffrage. The national convention of the Alliance in August, 1914 declared against the Anti-Saloon League and also the "equally obnoxious advocates of female suffrage."[28] Letters were circulated in German to the German citizens and local alliances. They appealed to German nationalism, urged them to stand together and to oppose woman suffrage, which was only intended to saddle the "yoke of prohibition" on their necks.[29] The Alliance was not entirely without grounds in linking suffrage with prohibition. After all, the Nebraska Prohibition Party included suffrage in its platforms continually from 1884 to 1920, and often they shared the same reformists. It also was not uncommon to hear a suffragist condemning the evil and drunkenness in this male—ruled world or singing "Many a laddie votes his ballot/Overcome with RYE."

Actually, it was not the principles of the Anti's that hurt the suffragists, but their tactics. They cut into suffrage parades with suffrage-bannered cars intended to make the suffragettes look foolish. And at the last minute they circulated a tale concerning a woman locked up with eleven men for forty-eight hours while serving on a jury. "Men, do you want your Mother, Your wife, your daughter to serve on a jury? If not, vote no." In reality, suffrage would not have opened jury duty to women; nevertheless, Mrs. Katherine Sumney felt the most damage was done by this "terrible tale." "I shall always think our campaign was too 'ladylike.' Everyone was afraid to fight," she wrote.[30]

Suffragists refused to give up, however, even if their ladylike fighting postponed the victory. Activities included taking over the Legislature after it adjourned sine die (in which they showed their skill and efficiency), invading a boiler factory with their petitions or crusading to nearby towns. One suffragette "blithely joined in a crusade to Lincoln, forgetting her husband entirely. Not only did he miss supper, but he had no idea where she had gone."[31]

Headlines of 1915 described the failure of another municipal suffrage bill, the winning of converts for suffrage by the eloquence of William Jennings Bryan and the Rev, Billy Sunday, and the organizing of the Nebraska Suffrage Pig Committee. The chairman, Mrs. Harriet C. King, urged suffragists to "Bring on your pigs!" The fat of these sacrificial pigs was converted into money for the campaign.[32] Other sources of revenue were donations, bazaars and the sale of old rags, papers, bones and rubber.

Then came 1917 and what seemed to be just another municipal suffrage bill. It passed the House easily with a vote of seventy-three to twenty-four. But Senate power was in the hands of two German-American politicians (John Mattes and Philip Kohl), and the bill died in committee. It would have met the fate of previous suffrage bills had not another bill appeared, a repeal of a law requiring that German be taught in grade schools whenever a designated number of people requested it. The Alliance made a deal: municipal suffrage in exchange for defeat of the repeal. Suffragists agreed and rejoiced that they now could vote for all offices not mentioned in the constitution, i.e. city and county officials and presidential electors. "With this good beginning," stated Mrs. W. E. Barkley, president of the Nebraska Woman's Suffrage Association, "the women of Nebraska hope to complete the work by getting full suffrage in 1918."

"We will call in suffragists from Colorado and Wyoming on the west, from Dakota and Minnesota on the north and northeast, from Iowa and Missouri on the east and southeast, and from Kansas on the south.... [to] help carry Nebraska for woman suffrage..."[33]

Success was short-lived. No sooner was the bill signed than Senator Mattes headed a group to circulate a petition seeking annulment of the new statute. In less than a month, the Alliance and other Anti's had obtained the necessary signatures, filed a referendum and suspended operation of the suffrage law. The suffragists contested the petition immediately, and investigation found one-third to one-half of the signatures the result of fraud, forgery and

misrepresentation. After two years of an exhausting court battle, Judge Leonard Flansburg declared the petition invalid.[34] Riding on the heels of the national suffrage amendment, this municipal suffrage law was too late to aid its original purpose. It did, however, become important in other ways.

First, "the case" won national attention. The Woman Citizen claimed "no battle for suffrage was ever fought harder than this legal battle in Nebraska."[35] Suffragists in every state awaited the outcome and helped to support their Nebraska friends. (The examining of witnesses often cost the Suffrage Association $150 a day.) Secondly, the Anti's had to pay the court costs, totaling several thousand dollars. They also lost considerable influence because of their dishonesty. Finally, the 1917 case had demonstrated weaknesses in the referendum law and brought about needed changes. The solicitor of petition signers, for example, must now live in the county in which he works.

The close of an era was rapidly coming. A full suffrage amendment was introduced in the Senate in March of 1919, but Mrs. Barkley requested withdrawal "because a new constitution will be submitted to the voters in 1920."[36] A few months later, the Federal Congress passed the Nineteenth Amendment, and the Nebraska Legislature accepted it unanimously.[37]

On August 2, 1919, Nebraska became the fourteenth state to ratify the amendment. In commemoration of this event, Governor Samuel R. McKelvie addressed the people, telling them to "rejoice and break forth into singing." He also recommended that "September twenty-eight be observed as a day for general celebration, and that at twelve o'clock high noon, let all the bells ring out the old and ring in the new."[38]

A new age had indeed begun. In 1920 the Nebraska Woman Suffrage Association reorganized as the Nebraska League of Women Voters, and the women prepared to exercise their first voting privileges. It had taken sixty—five years to achieve this victory. Men were still everywhere—but no longer alone.

This article appeared in the Summer 1968 issue of Nebraska History *with this author bio: "Mrs. Wilhite is a 1967 graduate of Midland Lutheran College in Fremont. Her article was written while she was a student at Midland."*

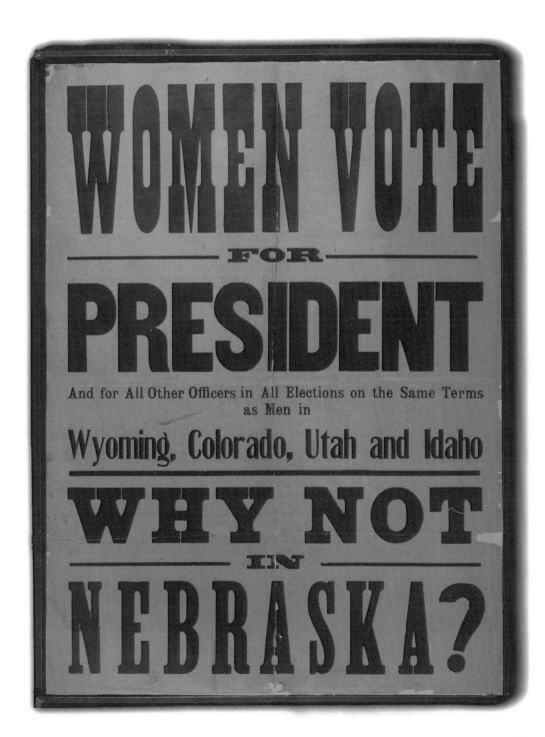

When this poster was printed, women had gained full voting rights in four states: Wyoming (1890 as a state; 1869 as a territory); Colorado (1893); Utah (1896 as a state; 1870 as a territory); and Idaho (1896). Washington would be next in 1910. HN RG2669-14.

Susan B. Anthony
and the Abbott Sisters
by David L. Bristow

I n the twentieth century two sisters from Grand Island rose to national prominence as social workers and reformers. Grace and Edith Abbott had a lasting impact on issues such as child labor and children's rights, immigration, and social security. They were also professional pioneers, heading the US Department of Labor's Children's Bureau (Grace) and serving as the first woman dean of a graduate school in an American university and the first dean of the first school of social work in the nation (Edith). "The Abbott Sisters," as they are often known, are among the most admired women in Nebraska history; Grace was inducted into the Nebraska Hall of Fame in 1976.

It seems fitting, then, that as children the sisters crossed paths with the famous suffragist Susan B. Anthony. They could thank their parents for that.

Othman Abbott settled in Grand Island after his service in the Civil War. He became an attorney and was elected Nebraska's first lieutenant governor (1877-79). He married Elizabeth in 1873 and shared with her an interest in women's rights.[1] In his 1929 book, *Recollections of a Pioneer Lawyer*, Othman recalled that his wife "had been brought up by her mother, her Aunt Lydia, and her Uncle Allen Gardner to be one of the early advocates of 'women's rights.' She and I had sent back and forth before our marriage John Stuart Mill's *Subjection of Women* and one of our daughters still preserves the copy with our marginal notes in it. We were both very hopeful when the Legislature of Nebraska finally submitted a woman suffrage amendment to the state Constitution in 1882. Mrs. Abbott became one of the officers of the Nebraska Woman Suffrage Society, and we both worked in the local campaign."[2]

Susan B. Anthony—who at that time was one of two vice presidents of the National Woman Suffrage Association—was deeply interested in the Nebraska campaign. Anthony expressed her hope and enthusiasm in a letter to Elizabeth Abbott that is preserved in History Nebraska's Abbott Family collection:

Rochester N.Y. Aug. 22, 1881

My Dear "Little Boss"—

The tables are turning – but not toward Vinemont[3] – Mrs Stanton[4] has surrendered to Malarial Fever – and thus cut off – or set back our history project of getting Vol. 2d done by the Holidays – So I am planning to rush into County Conventions in Western New York – to rouse the women to seize their School Suffrage duty this fall - - So that cuts Vinemont meeting you see –

And then I am thinking away from the Southern Sweep next February and March – I'll tell you why – because in November 1882 the men of Nebraska are to say yea or nay to allowing the women of that state to vote – and, hence, that it is our duty as the National Mother to put all our forces into Nebraska from immediately after our Wash. Con. up to their election – even to holding our May Anniversary at its Capital – Lincoln – who shall say – that by this swooping down upon that one state – we might not carry at least one man more than half to vote "For Woman suffrage"— and if we could – what a triumph it would be!! – Isn't that our duty as a National Soul – to help actively, wherever the question is brought to a practical test? – You see neither Indiana nor Oregon can be certain of carrying the question to a vote – until their next Legislatures shall satisfy the proposition – and

they will not meet until 1882 – hence will not vote till Nov. 1882 – So you see if we could sweep into Nebraska with such a power as to knock down that one brick – get suffrage there – it would be easy to sweep Oregon & Indiana the next year – I did not believe it possible for me to get up so much hope of success of a popular vote of any state – But the women of Nebraska are so alive – & so many of their newspapers have come out for Woman suffrage – that I cannot help like the old war horse – to be roused to life – & so I propose that we all turn in & work in Nebraska – concentrate there – & see what will come of it – you see – if we could get U.S. Senators & MCs.[5] from one state who had to look to women for their laurels – we should have so many fine friends in Congress – with Love to N___ a & ____ & ever so much for your own dear self.

Affectionately yours – S. B. Anthony[6]

Othman Abbott described what happened as the campaign heated up in 1882:

"Miss Anthony travelled out to Nebraska herself that year and we were happy when she stayed at our house and spoke at a public meeting in Grand Island. It was a very splendid meeting for those days and Miss Anthony herself seemed pleased with it. I ought to chronicle one remark she made after she had shaken hands with the last person in the audience who lingered to meet her or talk with her. Mrs. Abbott said as we walked away that it must be very hard to have to shake hands with so many people. Miss Anthony replied as quick as a flash, 'Oh, my dear, if you could only know how much easier it is today to shake hands with people than it was in the old days when no one wanted to shake hands with me!'

"Miss Anthony also helped the cause greatly by sending us a very fine German woman speaker, Mrs. Clara Neyman [Newman]. She came, I believe, from Brooklyn, New York, and she did good work among those who could only be reached in the German language. Mrs. Neyman also stayed at our house, and we enjoyed her visit also. I ought to add that our house was rather crowded then and while Mrs. Neyman was there and one night while Miss

Anthony was there the only way we could manage was to have our little daughter Edith, six years old, used as a bed fellow. She was very proud of it, particularly of sleeping with Miss Anthony."[7]

That fall, Nebraska stood on the verge of becoming the first state to give women the vote. But as Kristin Mapel Bloomberg explains in the following article, the campaign failed, prompting Anthony to rethink her national strategy.

Previous Page: Susan B. Anthony sat for this portrait in Nebraska City during an 1871 visit. HN RG2669-5

Below Left: Image of Elizabeth Abbott. HN RG2411-5

Below Right: O.A. Abbott, husband of Elizabeth Abbott. HN RG2916-11

Opposite: Letter from Susan B. Anthony to Elizabeth Abbott. A slogan on the letterhead reads: "'Governments derive their just powers from the consent of the governed;' the ballot is consent. Why should woman be governed without her consent?" HN RG2916.AM

Rochester N. Y. Aug. 22. 1881

My dear "Little Boss" —

The tables are turning — but not toward Ninemont — Mrs Stanton has surrendered to Malarial fever — and thus cut off — a set back our history project — of getting vol. 2d done by the holidays — So I am planing to rush into County Conventions in western New york — to urge the women to seize their School Suffrage duty this fall — So that cuts Ninemont meeting you see —

And there I am thinking away from the Southern Sweep next February & March — I'll tell you why — because in November the men of Nebraska are to decide the way to allowing the women of that state to vote — and, hence, that it is our force to National Mother to put all our force into Nebraska — from immediately after our Wash. Con. up to their election, — even to

"Striving for Equal Rights for All":
Woman Suffrage in Nebraska 1855-1882
by Kristin Mapel Bloomberg

Three times prior to the twentieth century, Nebraska women stood on the threshold of full citizenship, and three times their efforts were denied. Like any social movement, the nearly century-long struggle for woman's rights was made up of local failures and achievements, both of which helped propel the national movement forward. And while Nebraska's early suffrage initiatives failed, they were key historical moments that shaped the trajectory of the national women's rights movement that ultimately led to a strategy to amend the United States Constitution. In other words, after striking out in Nebraska three times in thirty years, many woman suffrage advocates decided that state legislative change—even in progressive states—was better left behind in favor of national legislative change....[1]

As a result of Nebraska's quickly changing demographics, the work done by national activists in the early 1870s was largely forgotten. But in the late 1870s, a grassroots movement for woman suffrage emerged from southeast Nebraska, generally organized by newcomers to the state, who Lucy Correll of Hebron called a "band of progressive, thinking women" residing in Gage, Douglas, Jefferson, Polk, and Thayer counties.[2] These women were broadminded and educated civic activists married to progressive and politically active men; among them were Clara Bewick Colby, whose husband Leonard W. Colby was a well-known Beatrice attorney; Lucy Correll, whose husband Erasmus M. Correll was editor of the *Hebron Journal*; Harriet S. Brooks, whose husband D. C.

Left: Clara Bewick Colby's efforts to organize a suffrage movement in Nebraska impressed national leaders such as Susan B. Anthony. Colby, however, knew that the local movement had deep roots. "It is remarkable," she wrote in the 1880s, that thirty years earlier "in a country with but scant communication with the older parts of the Republic, this instinctive justice should have crystallized into legislative action." Wisconsin Historical Society, Image ID: 26613

Opposite: Ada M. Bittenbender became editor of Nebraska's first Farmer's Alliance newspaper. She served as an attorney for the Woman's Christian Temperance Union and in 1888 was admitted to argue cases before the United States Supreme Court. *The New Republic* (Lincoln), Aug. 23, 1888.

The morning of November 7, 1882, was far from an ordinary morning in Nebraska. It was Election Day, and a special one at that. Nebraska was poised to become the first state in the Union to recognize women's right to full suffrage and equal citizenship with men. It was a moment nearly thirty years in the making and a result both of Nebraska's history of progressivism and of a serendipitous convergence of people and politics. Women's rights advocates hoped to transform national politics by changing their state constitution, but they were to be disappointed.

Brooks was editor of the *Omaha Republican*; and Ada M. Bittenbender, who with her husband H. C. Bittenbender, was editor of the *Osceola Record*.

This activism was in large part due to the personal experiences and networks brought by the core group of Ada M. Bittenbender, Harriet Brooks, Erasmus M. Correll, and Clara Bewick Colby. Their shared values regarding political philosophy and education, as well as their professional experience, united them—as did their understanding of the West as a place of social transformation and political opportunity that could be used to build a better America. Brooks (b. 1828), the most senior of Nebraska's woman's rights activists, was college-educated and raised in Michigan, and had experience in Chicago's Cook County Woman's Franchise Association and the Illinois Woman's Suffrage Association, as well as the National Woman Suffrage Association.[3] She arrived in Nebraska in 1876 when her husband accepted the editorship of the *Omaha Republican*. Bittenbender (b. 1848) was also college-educated, and gained distinction as Nebraska's first "lady lawyer." With her husband, she emigrated from Pennsylvania to Osceola, Nebraska in 1878, where Henry Bittenbender began practicing law and in 1879 purchased and Ada began editing the *Osceola Record*. Ada Bittenbender, with her husband, later established the Polk County Agricultural Association, and became editor of the first Farmers' Alliance newspaper in Nebraska. A temperance advocate, she was an influential member of the Nebraska Woman's Christian Temperance Union, who in 1888 was admitted to argue cases before the United States Supreme Court and served as the attorney for the National WCTU.[4]

But among this group, Clara Colby and Erasmus Correll could be counted as particularly influential during this crucial time. Correll (b. 1846) was a college-educated newspaperman who moved to Nebraska from Illinois in 1869. In 1871 Correll established the *Hebron Journal*, which immediately gained a reputation as a newspaper favorable to woman's rights. During 1881 and 1882, he edited and published the *Western Woman's Journal*, which served as the organ of the Nebraska Woman Suffrage Association and was the first woman suffrage paper in the state. He was elected from Thayer County to the Nebraska House of Representatives in 1880, and as a result of that

position, introduced the bill for woman suffrage that was the focus of the Nebraska campaign in 1881 and 1882.[5] Lucy Correll worked on both of her husband's newspapers, and was instrumental in establishing the first permanent woman suffrage association in Nebraska.

———————

Like the others in this group, Colby (b. 1846) was college educated. Raised on the Wisconsin frontier, she moved to Beatrice, Nebraska, in 1872 with her husband, Leonard Wright Colby, who set up a thriving legal practice. In 1876, Leonard purchased the *Beatrice Express*, the town's Republican newspaper, and became its editor and proprietor; Clara later contributed columns.[6] In 1877, Leonard Colby was elected a Nebraska state senator. With the other Nebraska suffrage leaders, Clara Colby shared a passion for civic improvement, society building, and newspapering. In Nebraska she threw herself into public life, where she worked to establish the Beatrice Public Library, engaged speakers of national reputation for the Ladies' Literary Association, served as the principal of the Beatrice Public School District, assisted with Correll's *Western Woman's Journal*, and later edited and published the *Woman's Tribune* (1883-1909), which was second woman suffrage paper in Nebraska and the second-longest-running woman suffrage paper in the United States.[7]

A number of common characteristics unified these Nebraska suffrage leaders, and may account for the revitalized effort for woman suffrage. Three of the four came of age on America's emerging Western frontier: Correll in Illinois, Brooks in Michigan, and Colby in Wisconsin. All earned college degrees, and shared a similar European Protestant heritage. Correll, Colby, and Bittenbender were of the same generation, and as adults all worked in the educated professional class and lived in town. None were wealthy; their economic position is best classified as middle class. In addition, the three women each had ties to national progressive women's networks. For example, Bittenbender was active in the Woman's Christian Temperance Union, Colby was active in the Association for the Advancement of Women, and Brooks had ties to the National Woman Suffrage Association. But importantly, this group held passionate views about frontier America; their interest was driven by a Turnerian sense of American progress, social idealism, and sense of responsibility in helping to create a better society as it was being constructed in the West.[8] With other progressives who settled Nebraska, they held the distinct view that they were there to help build up a good society, not take profit from it. Thus, their personal experiences, political beliefs, and extended networks helped prime the pump for a revitalized focus on woman suffrage in Nebraska.

As the local movement gained momentum, Nebraska suffrage activists rediscovered Susan B. Anthony, who accepted Erasmus Correll's invitation to lecture in Hebron on the topic "Bread versus the Ballot" on October 30, 1877.[9] Significantly, now it was Nebraska advocates seeking the assistance of national workers, not the other way around, and the early work done by the Corrells, Colby, and others had shaped a constituency ready to hear Anthony's message. Her talk electrified the cause because, Lucy Correll explains, "Previous to this time many self-satisfied women believed they had all the 'rights' they wanted, but they were soon awakened to

a new consciousness of their true status wherein they discovered their 'rights' were only 'privileges.'"[10] As the *Western Woman's Journal* reported, Anthony "aroused the community, and a majority of the leading citizens became converts to the doctrine of equal rights."[11]

Colby scheduled Anthony to speak in Beatrice the day following her lecture in Hebron. Anthony declared the stop in Beatrice a resounding success, and was impressed with Colby's feminist activism which she acknowledged in a letter written from Lincoln while waiting for the next leg of her journey:

> Such women as you . . . have <u>individual work to do</u> —to lift the world into better conditions— & I hope you will not allow anything to estop *[sic]* you from doing what seems to be your duty— I long to see women <u>be themselves</u> —not the <u>mere echoes of men</u>— . . . Mrs. Colby—do, please, write a brief letter of <u>your</u> library work—& lecture Course for the <u>December</u> number of the Ballot Box. . . For you— & every woman to tell what you are doing—helps to rouse other women to do likewise— Women want to be helped into the feeling that they <u>can</u> help on the good works they like to see done— We have been told we

Opposite Left: Lucy Correll of Hebron wrote for her husband's pro-suffrage newspapers and was instrumental in establishing the first permanent woman suffrage association in Nebraska. HN RG2411-1106

Opposite Right: Erasmus M. Correll, Lucy's husband, founded the *Hebron Journal* in 1871. It soon gained a reputation as a newspaper favorable to women's rights. In 1881-1882, he published and edited the *Western Woman's Journal*, Nebraska's first suffrage paper. HN RG2141-512

Opposite Far Left: The November 1, 1877, issue of the *Hebron Journal* reported Susan B. Anthony's lecture there a few days earlier.

Opposite Background: Erasmus M. Correll was adept at using the *Hebron Journal* to unite a far-flung frontier constituency sympathetic to the cause of women's rights. In doing so, he began to develop a more comprehensive state suffrage movement.

THE HEBRON JOURNAL.

"Forward, Fearless and Free."

| ESTABLISHED MARCH, 1871. |

VOL. VII, NO. 19.   **HEBRON, NEB., THURSDAY, NOV. 1, 1877.**   **WHOLE NO. 331.**

SUSAN B. ANTHONY.

THE lecture by Susan B. Anthony, Tuesday night, on the subject, "Woman wants Bread, not the Ballot," was a clear, logical, and masterly exposition of the theory known as "woman's rights."

The firm, massive under jaw of the lady is indicative of the stern will that has actuated her in her long battle in behalf of her sex, given her the title of "the invincible," and inscribed her name in imperishable characters on the summit of the rugged mount of fame.

couldn't do anything but help the individual man or men of our families—So long & so constantly—that very few women can of themselves get into any work above that—[12]

By praising Colby's public reform efforts in Beatrice, and by asking her to submit pieces to the radical journal the *National Citizen and Ballot Box* (1878-1881), Anthony's request illustrates the importance assigned to journals and newspapers advocating the suffrage cause. In this way, Nebraskans framed their work as part of a larger social effort, thus uniting what might be seen as disparate local activities into those that furthered a structured, national plan.

Erasmus Correll was particularly adept at using the vehicle of the newspaper to unite a far-flung frontier constituency sympathetic to the cause of women's rights. In doing so, he began to develop a more comprehensive state suffrage movement—which had been lacking in previous attempts to pass woman suffrage legislation—by building on the political momentum gained by Anthony's visit. In early 1879, Correll established a woman's column in his newspaper the *Hebron Journal*, and was thus able to further the discussion of woman's rights by publishing—often on the front page—articles written for a readership of women, on topics of interest to women, and usually signed by women writers. A range of topics from the column's first ten weeks were illustrative of those covered

during its multi-year run, and included articles on women and education, labor, and temperance; woman suffrage; a discussion of reading material appropriate for young women and girls; and a discussion of women's roles in the family.[13] Keen to encourage debate, Correll also printed the article, "From an Anti-Suffragist."[14] Thus, through the pages of the *Hebron Journal*, Correll began to build up a broad constituency supportive of woman's rights.[15]

Correll followed a pattern of igniting debate and continuing discussion in the pages of the *Journal* when in the spring of 1879 he extended an invitation to another national speaker—this time Elizabeth Cady Stanton.[16] Stanton's lecture topic was "Our Girls," which the *Hebron Journal* reported, had she lived in the Middle Ages, she "would have been burned at the stake as a martyr to advanced principles."[17] Nebraskans were ready to hear Stanton's radical woman's rights message; as a result, her presence in southeast Nebraska left a lasting mark on the Nebraska woman's rights movement. Following her address to the citizens of Hebron, Stanton led a private program for women which resulted in the organization of the Thayer County Woman's Suffrage Association—the first permanent woman suffrage association in the state of Nebraska, counting a total of fifteen members.[18]

The mission of that first association was "to secure State and National protection for women citizens in the exercises of their right to vote," and fewer than two months after its founding, its membership counted thirty-five women.[19] The Association immediately began

its work, and made its first project the circulation of a suffrage petition to be sent to the United States Congress.[20] In celebration of their organization, the women of Hebron declared Stanton their champion, which was noted in the *Hebron Journal*'s "Women's Column" on May 15, 1879:

> We congratulate the women that they have organized the Women's S[uffrage] A[ssociation] under such favorable circumstances. Whoever had the privilege of listening to Mrs. Stanton, enjoyed a "feast of reason and a flow of soul" . . . . Let us consider this matter carefully, not thinking of it lightly, as we would the organization of a newly formed social or [wife] society, but as something to mould and move the nation—a thing not of to-day, but for coming time. . . . Truly, as Mrs. Stanton said, we may be thankful to the editor of the JOURNAL for giving us the control of a column in his paper, a column devoted to the interests of women—a liberality not shown by many papers. This pioneer paper is opening the way. No doubt many will be ready to follow.21

Many did follow. Emulating the *Hebron Journal*'s 'Woman's Column," the following year saw other newspapers dedicate space to their own woman's columns

Top:
Hebron, Nebraska, in the 1870s, during the time that Erasmus and Lucy Correll were involved with the *Hebron Journal*. HN RG2719-8-3

Inset: Hebron, Nebraska, ca. 1870s. Thanks to the leadership of the Corrells, national suffrage leaders such as Susan B. Anthony and Elizabeth Cady Stanton lectured there, helping create momentum for the movement. HN RG2719-8-1

edited and written by Nebraska's female woman suffrage leaders whose political passion and strength of personality took them through the door opened by the *Hebron Journal*. These included columns in the *Beatrice Express*, edited by Clara Bewick Colby; in the *Omaha Republican*, edited by Harriet S. Brooks; in the *Osceola Record*, edited by Ada M. Bittenbender; and in the *Johnson County Journal*, edited by Lucinda Russell. The crown jewel of the Nebraska woman's rights campaign, however, was later set in the form of the *Western Woman's Journal*, established by Erasmus Correll in April 1881 as the first woman suffrage paper in Nebraska. Although its tenure was little more than a year and a half, the women's rights news contained within its pages solidified the suffrage movement in Nebraska and, Colby observed, "a host of women suddenly found themselves gifted with the power to speak and write, which they consecrated to the cause of

Western Woman's Journal.

"EQUALITY BEFORE THE LAW."—Motto of Nebraska.   AN ARISTOCRACY OF SEX IS REPUGNANT TO A REPUBLIC.

Vol. I.   LINCOLN, NEB., APRIL, 1881.   No. 1.

WESTERN WOMAN'S JOURNAL.

Devoted to Woman and her Home, Industrial, Educational, and Legal Interests—especially advocating Woman Suffrage.

ERASMUS M. CORRELL, Editor & Prop'r.

(Also Editor and Proprietor of the Hebron Journal.)

SUBSCRIPTION RATES:

One Year, in advance, $1.25
In Clubs of ten or more, per year,   1.00
    Sample Copies mailed on receipt of 10 cents.

Rates of Advertising furnished on application. Communications of all kinds to be addressed to the WESTERN WOMAN'S JOURNAL, Lincoln, Nebraska.

Registered at the Lincoln, Nebraska, Post-Office, as second-class mail matter.

OUR GREETING.

Without apology, with no plea for special consideration, we present to a critical public the first number of the WESTERN WOMAN'S JOURNAL. We sincerely believe its mission a noble one. Its aims, objects and tone, if not eloquently, are, at least, clearly and sharply defined on its pages. Whatever faults it has we hope to lessen—whatever merits it may possess we shall earnestly endeavor to increase. Such as it is, with a strong determination to make it better with each succeeding number, we send it forth. If it be unworthy of success, we shall receive without murmuring the adverse judgment—if it merit a favorable reception from a discriminating public, we shall gratefully appreciate the decision, and strive to attain a higher state of excellence and a corresponding degree of success.   ERASMUS M. CORRELL.

RIGHTS.

No subjects are of greater importance than questions affecting the political condition of the people. The mental, moral, and physical welfare of the citizens of a state or nation depend more upon the degree of liberty of thought and action enjoyed by the individual citizen than upon anything else.

By reason of the mere fact of existence, every human being possesses certain inherent personal rights. Among these are the right to live, the right to think and act, and the right of enjoyment. In addition to these, certain other rights belong to every human being not incapacitated by infancy, insanity, idiocy, or crime. Among these rights are the right to acquire and control property, the right to have and express opinions, and the right of a voice in the organization and management of such societies, associations or governments as may be organized to limit, restrict or control his or her personal rights or privileges.

These rights are not determined by the sex of the individual, nor are they dependent upon any other physical qualification or accident, but pertain equally to all persons. They are *birthrights* founded upon the broad *magna charta* of humanity, and are as inherent and indefeasible as the eternal and immutable principles of truth and justice are indestructible.

interests, to change or amend the constitution by which they are governed.

Governments which do not give just and equal protection and privileges to *all* citizens, fail to carry out the principles of true government.

The constitution of the state of Nebraska and the constitutions of the other states composing the Union do not provide for equal political rights to women, but authorize an aristocracy of sex, repugnant alike to natural right, justice and the principles of republican government. The educational, social, legal, industrial, and property rights of women depend, as do those of men, upon their political rights.

The ballot secures and protects these rights, and is the means by which people declare their will.

Those who advocate woman suffrage do not ask as a favor or privilege the removal of the unjust restrictions that now prevent women from receiving the just and equal benefits of citizenship. They ask for the ballot as a *right*, and maintain that by whatever tenures of right men hold the ballot, women claim it upon the same ground. Upon every basis of equity, of justice, and of a wise and enlightened public policy, the amendment to the constitution providing for equal political rights for women, should receive the sanction and support of all citizens who believe in progress as opposed to prejudice and injustice, and who have the best interests of the state at heart.

their civil liberties."[22]

As Nebraska women formally organized in support of woman suffrage and woman's rights, Harriet Brooks took action to create a state suffrage association in order to unite the variety of local associations springing up around the state. In her Omaha home on May 30, 1880, Brooks and a half-dozen other women including Clara Colby of Beatrice and Lucy Correll of Hebron met for the purpose of organizing an association to be known as the Nebraska State Suffrage Association. The organization itself was tentative, designed to begin a process that would be expanded later.[23] The main impetus of the meeting, however, was to appoint Brooks and one other as delegates to the mass meeting of the National Woman Suffrage Association in Chicago to be held in June 1880. Brooks's ties to both the NWSA and the Chicago associations would prove to be important connections now that Nebraska was ready to move forward with another challenge to the state's constitution.

———————

In the fall of 1880, two members of the Thayer County Woman Suffrage Association were elected to the Nebraska legislature: Erasmus Correll to the House of Representatives and his colleague Charles B. Coon to the Senate.[24] From these positions and backed by a growing grassroots support, Correll and Coon were in place to offer a constitutional question at Nebraska's sixteenth regular session of the legislature in 1881. Accordingly, Correll introduced Nebraska House Roll No. 162, a "Joint resolution providing for the submission to the electors of this state of an amendment to section 1, article 7, of the constitution,"[25] which aimed to strike the word "male" from the Suffrage article of the Nebraska constitution of 1875 and replace it with the word "person."

With growing public attention to the suffrage issue as a result of the planned introduction of House Roll 162, interest developed in creating a formal statewide woman suffrage association beyond the scope of the tentative one formed in Omaha in May 1880. Noting the urgency of gathering organized support, Lucinda Russell of Tecumseh issued this call in Harriet Brooks's column in the *Omaha Republican*:

> We think it best to call a meeting, even now at this somewhat late day, and send women to Lincoln who will attend personally to this matter. We have left these things neglected too long. Will you call on all women of the State who can do so to assemble at Lincoln during the session of the legislature, appointing the day, etc.? I think we would be surprised at the result. This town contains scarcely a woman who is opposed to woman suffrage. We know we are a power here; and we do not know but the same hearty support which Tecumseh would afford may exist in many towns through the State. All we need for good earnest work and mighty results is organization.[26]

As the legislature began to meet in January, Nebraska women convened in Lincoln, and on January 27, 1881, the Nebraska Woman Suffrage Association was formally organized with Harriet Brooks at the helm, and representation from each judicial district in the state.[27] The Nebraska WSA immediately turned its attention to supporting Correll's bill and, Colby explained, "Headquarters were established in Lincoln. Mrs. Brooks remained during the session, and Mesdames Holmes, Russell, Dinsmoor and Colby all, or most of the time, until the act was passed, interviewing the members and securing the promise of their votes for the measure."[28]

Critical to securing passage of the amendment was getting voices of its beneficiaries heard by the legislature—this had not been done in a meaningful way during the prior two attempts for woman suffrage. To this end, testimony before the legislature was given by Harriet Brooks, Orpha Dinsmoor, Clara Colby and others who detailed support from all corners of the state. As Colby explained, "Though we who are present are few in numbers, we know that the desire in the section from which we come is very great that this measure be submitted to the people. I may [say] that the ladies in my own town are nearly unanimous in favor of the suffrage for women." Brooks noted the support of "many

Opposite: Erasmus Correll established *The Western Woman's Journal* in Lincoln in 1881. It promoted suffrage and other women's interests. HN RG1073

prominent men and women throughout the state," and singled out "reports from every section of 'a constant pressure' for this measure." She explained, "The question had passed beyond trifling and ridicule many years ago; and it has now almost passed beyond the necessity of argument." Dinsmoor seconded Brooks, noting, "Many ladies of Omaha said to me before coming: 'Tell the members of the legislature that we want a voice.' . . . . while woman has been knocking at the door, the black man has received the suffrage—and justly and rightfully, too, for his own protection as a free citizen. It has now come to the question of absolute right—whether one class of people shall say to another: 'You can come only thus far in the direction of liberty.'"[29]

But for women like Colby, woman suffrage reflected the best tenets of western life that placed the building of state and society on the shoulders of equally hard-working and patriotic women and men:

> The sentiment in many parts of the east, among the learned and society classes is strongly in favor of this, but in the west we have the heart of the people. . . . In the east— as in Massachusetts, where there are 100,000 more women than men—the men seem more tenacious of their rights. Here there is no such sentiment, for there is no occasion for it. Indeed, we women consider ourselves pioneers, equally with our brothers and husbands, and we know that we are helping build up the state in equal measure with you. We, like you, are proud of this state, of our state, and we wish perfect liberty to help you build it up in all that is befitting a great and good commonwealth.[30]

For Colby, then, the question of woman suffrage had already been answered by the people of Nebraska who viewed themselves as pioneers—both on the prairies and in politics. Suffrage, then, was a right earned by those who would use it to further the best interests of their chosen state, bestowed equally upon women who worked shoulder to shoulder with men and had gained their respect.

The bill passed and was signed by the governor on February 26, 1881.[31] With legislative approval secured,

the Nebraska Woman Suffrage Association swung into action with the monumental goal of passing the state suffrage amendment when it came before the electorate in November 1882, giving them less than two years to campaign. From February to July 1881, efforts focused on building an educated popular voter base. As Colby explains, "Lectures were given, and societies and working committees formed as rapidly as possible."[32] By the time the Thayer County Woman's Suffrage Association celebrated its second anniversary in the spring of 1881, thirty-nine Nebraska woman's rights associations had been created across the state, including the Nebraska Woman's Suffrage Association, nine county associations and twenty-nine local associations.[33] And by the time the Governor's proclamation announcing the vote on the amendment was published in the *Western Woman's Journal* in September 1882, more than 175 woman suffrage associations were active in Nebraska.[34]

While Wyoming Territory had granted women full suffrage in 1869 and Utah Territory in 1870,[35] no state had yet done so, and Nebraska was now poised to become the first. Next on the suffragists' agenda was the organization of the first general convention of the Nebraska Woman Suffrage Association held in Omaha in July 1881, which attracted many of the leading women and men citizens of Omaha who listened to speeches such as Ada M. Bittenbender's "Legal Disabilities of the Women of Nebraska," and a lively debate between Clara Colby and Edward Rosewater, the prominent anti-suffragist editor of the *Omaha Bee*.[36] But the main business of the convention was the adoption of convention resolutions—worthy daughters of the 1848 Seneca Falls convention:

> Resolved, Than an aristocracy of sex is inconsistent with republican principles.
> Resolved, That the fundamental principles of our American republic are:
> First—"Government derives its just powers from the consent of the governed";
> Second— That "Taxation and representation are inseparable"; as woman is governed and as woman is taxed, woman is clearly entitled to a voice in the government and representation in the halls of the legislature; and that the constitution in prohibiting woman suffrage, not only violates natural rights, but is equally

antagonistic to itself.

    Resolved, That the act of men in continuing the disfranchisement of one-half of the citizens of this commonwealth, is an unwarranted use of power no longer to be patiently tolerated.

    Resolved, That as long as woman is unjustly withheld from exercising her right of suffrage, she should not be held answerable to the laws nor subject to taxation.

    Resolved, That the abridging of woman's right to hold office and have trial by a jury of her peers, is a tyrannical exercise of power.

    Resolved, That the most unjust distinction is made in the statutes of Nebraska in favor of man; Therefore, we urgently request the legislature, at its next session, to reconstruct the laws, doing away with all discrimination between the sexes.

    Resolved, That it is clearly the duty of the women of Nebraska to become intelligently acquainted with the laws by which they are governed; that the apathy of woman in regard to the wrongs of her sex, instead of being a plea for remaining in her present condition, is the strongest argument against it. . . .

    Resolved, That we pledge ourselves not to relinquish our untiring efforts to wipe out forever the stigma of aristocracy of sex.[37]

Following the adoption of these resolutions, the convention continued its program of speeches and addresses that included "a masterly constitutional argument" from Clara Colby, and two speeches by Amelia Bloomer, who 'gave reminiscences of her work in the Nebraska Legislature twenty years ago," and another "reviewing the position of the Bible on the subjugation of women."[38]

In the same way Nebraskans used newspapers, conventions were an important way to excite and inform the electorate, and this first state convention paved the way for a third general convention and first delegate convention held later that year at Kearney in October, where the faithful were sustained with speeches and a reaffirmation of the resolutions adopted at July's convention in Omaha. The most important work of this convention however, was adopting the woman suffrage platform:

    We, the representatives of the Nebraska State Woman Suffrage Association, in convention assembled at Kearney, Nebraska, October 19th, '81, hereby declare our fealty to the great principles on which our government is founded, and reiterate the principles of the National Woman Suffrage Association . . . whose object is to secure to woman political equality with man.

    Contemplating these facts and mindful of the blessings we enjoy, we here earnestly resolve to continue the struggle for the supremacy of the right and the abolition of all wrong; trusting, hoping and striving for equal rights for all, and the lifting of the yoke of bondage from the oppressed of every class, sex and condition in life, and to this end we pledge our solemn determination to prosecute this effort until a satisfactory result is reached; and that our declared purpose shall continue to be the removal of all social, moral and political distinctions that to-day discriminate unjustly between the sexes and consecrate our lives and united energies to the ultimate adoption of the proposed constitutional amendment securing to the women of Nebraska the right of franchise.39

The Kearney convention also made clear that interest in the amendment was rising. As the *Western Woman's Journal* reported: "As illustrative of how much in earnest some of the Nebraska women are, we note that one lady, in order to attend the convention, rode thirty-five miles in a lumber wagon and another rode forty miles on a load of wheat."[40]

Nebraska suffragists understood the importance of their bill to national politics; they also understood that valuable political capital could be gained by connecting their work to both the American Woman Suffrage Association (AWSA) and the National Woman Suffrage Association (NWSA), the two national organizations focused on achieving woman suffrage.[41] Drawing support from both the AWSA and the NWSA would bring not only resources, but also national attention to their cause. And while the two associations enjoyed a strong rivalry, Nebraskans believed all might profit by setting aside differences to work together for the common goal of seeing the state become the first to recognize woman suffrage.

Only days after the Kearney convention, Erasmus Correll, Clara Colby and Lucinda Russell boarded a train to attend the eleventh annual meeting of the AWSA in Louisville, Kentucky, October 26 and 27, hoping to strengthen ties to the national movement. To their great surprise, Correll was unanimously elected president of the American Woman Suffrage Association, while Colby was elected a vice president serving Nebraska. Russell, by virtue of her delegate status, was appointed the Nebraska member to the AWSA Executive Committee.[42] The three returned to Nebraska to great acclaim, having had their efforts marked by a national body, thus adding greater emphasis to their work.

But unlike the early support offered by the AWSA, the NWSA remained cautious. Anthony, who had been observing these devel-opments from the sidelines, cautioned Correll:

Allow me to congratulate Nebraska generally, and yourself particularly on the honor of the Presidency of the American Woman Suffrage Association, conferred upon you at the recent Louisville Convention. I hope with the office and honor will go to Nebraska lots of money to help you carry forward . . . . I am hoping to see the end of [my current work] by May, so that I can give personal thought and work to Nebraska, for I feel the importance

Left: The most senior of Nebraska women's rights activists, Harriet Sophia Brewer Brooks had experience in suffrage organizations before arriving in Nebraska in 1876. Her ties to the National Woman Suffrage Association and the Chicago associations would prove important to the Nebraska movement. HN RG2411-620

Center: Susan B. Anthony (seated) and Clara Bewick Colby (right) continued working together long after the Nebraska suffrage initiative failed. In 1890 they and sculptor Bessie Potter sat for a portrait at Mathew Brady's studio in Washington, D.C. Sophia Smith Collection, Smith College Archives

Right: Edward Rosewater, the anti-suffragist editor of the *Omaha Daily Bee*, debated Clara Bewick Colby in 1881 and Susan B. Anthony in 1882. HN RG2411

of making the vote there as large as possible, though, after my experience in Kansas, Michigan, and Colorado, in each of which (of the two first at least) our hopes were as bright, seemingly, as are yours to-day. The difficulty is that the men who will vote no neither go out to lectures nor read tracts or newspapers. They cannot be reached by our educational instrumentalities—they are amenable only to bribes and bitters, neither, nor both of which can we stoop to. . . . such men are not earnest on our side, but intensely against us—every one—because they know their own mothers, wives, sisters, and daughters would vote down the three great pet institutions of such men—grog shops, brothels, and gambling houses. Still I cannot but hope for Nebraska.[43]

While she remained cautiously optimistic, Anthony's concern about the influence of the powerful liquor lobby, which vehemently opposed woman suffrage on the grounds that women would use the vote to prohibit the sale of liquor, was well founded in light of Nebraska's

Brady, WASHINGTON

Woman Suffrage.

SUPPLEMENT.

...e the Ballot should b...

believe the Ballot should be given

Women of Nebraska.

No. or
...oute   Town

AS IN NAME. NEBRASKA'S MOTTO: "EQUALITY BEFORE THE LAW."

chamber we should throw the windows wide open, and the sweet summer air would sweep all impurity away and fill our lungs with fresher life. If we would purge politics let us turn upon them the great stream of the purest human influence we know."

Women's presence at the polls and political meetings will greatly tend to preserve order and decorum and to insure a "free ballot and a fair count." Neither bayonets nor deputy sheriffs will be needed where wives and mothers are.

The licentiousness of our cities is largely due to the starvation pay of women dependent upon their own work for bread or by the death or misfortune...

WOMAN SUFFRAGE A POLITICAL REFORM.

Extract from an Address by Hon. H. B. Blackwell.

All admit that some change in our political system is needed. The growing corruption of public life is admitted and deplored by both parties. Low as is the average standard of private morals, the standard of political ethics is confessedly far lower every year matters seem to grow worse. Our laws and our law-makers do not represent the public sentiment of the community. * * * what shall we do about it? How ... cope with these stern facts? How

The Influence of Suffrage Upon Women Themselves.

Men complain of the ignorance, frivolity and apathy in the great questions of the day among women, and use the very fact as an objection against giving them suffrage. True, but their position has made them so. What incentive has any woman to interest herself in political subjects, in social economy, or in the great questions of the day, when the profoundest thought, the most logical reasoning, or the most able methods, if emanating from a woman's brain, are considered no better than the ravings of a maniac, or any more to be considered than the criminal's muttered oaths, for at the ballot box, the only place where thought ...

BISHOP SIMPSON: "I be... vices in our large cities will ... quered until the ballot is ... hands of women."

REV. JAMES FREEMAN CL... not think our politics will ... ought to be till women are l... voters."

GEORGE WILLIAM CUR... have quite as much interes... essment as men, and I hav... or read of any satisfactory ... cluding them from the ball... no more doubt of their ame... ence upon politics than I f... ... they exert everywhere

HERBERT SPENCER: "E... ... of political no...

The Woman's Tribune.

"EQUALITY BEFORE THE LAW."

Vol. V.   WASHINGTON, D. C., TUESDAY MARCH 27, 1888.   No. 16

THE WOMAN'S TRIBUNE,
Official Organ of the International Council.
Edited and Published Daily by
CLARA BEWICK COLBY
FOR THE
NATIONAL WOMAN SUFFRAGE ASSOCIATION.
WASHINGTON, D. C.

Terms: 5 cents a Copy; 35 cents a week.

Forty Years Ago.

Although references to the occasion of which this International Council of Women is the celebration are made in the President's address and touched upon by many of the speakers, it is fitting, since this is destined to be an historical event of momentous import, to take a backward look at this memorable convention and at an incident which was its immediate inspiration.

Elizabeth Cady had from childhood keenly felt the injustice of woman's position. As a girl she had studied Latin and Greek with the boys, and had taken prizes over them at the village academy. Then they had bade her farewell for the college, while the only opportunity open to her was a young ladies' seminary where she could learn French and dancing. This was such a sore disappointment that to-day she cannot recall it without bitter regret. She had studied jurisprudence in her father's office and knew that both by common law and statute woman was without...

such principles and organizing its powers in such form as to them shall seem most likely to effect their safety and happiness. Prudence, indeed, will dictate that governments long established should not be changed for light and transient causes, and accordingly all experience hath shown that mankind are more disposed to suffer, while evils are sufferable, than to right themselves by abolishing the forms to which they were accustomed. But when a long train of abuses and usurpations, pursuing invariably the same object evinces a design to reduce them under absolute despotism, it is their duty to throw off such government, and to provide new guards for their future security. Such has been the patient sufferance of the women under this Government, and such is now the necessity which constrains them to demand the equal station to which they are entitled.

The history of mankind is a history of repeated injuries and usurpations on the part of man toward woman, having in direct object the establishment of an absolute tyranny over her. To prove this, let facts be submitted to a candid world.

He has never permitted her to exercise her inalienable right to the elective franchise.

McClintock, Amy Post, Catharine A. F. Stebbins and others, and were adopted:

WHEREAS, The great precept of nature is conceded to be, that "man shall pursue his own true and substantial happiness." Blackstone in his Commentaries remarks, that this law of nature being coeval with mankind and dictated by God himself, is of course superior in obligation to any other. It is binding over all the globe, in all countries and at all ...

THE SUFFRAGISTS.

Lively Proceedings at the Morning Session of the Convention.

Obstreperous Males Can be Talked to Death

If They Cannot Be Convinced

After the battle in the opera house last night, and a gentle repose in the arms of Morpheus, the ladies of the National Suffrage association met at Boyd's opera house at 9:30 a. m., looking much refreshed. The rain had ceased early this morning, and by 8 o'clock the clouds began to disappear and few broken gleams of sunlight soon dried up the sidewalks. The suffragists lost none of their zeal by the skirmish with the young limb of the law last night, but on the contrary they had determination vividly portrayed upon their countenances and a relentless warfare

...Whittier.
...spire hope.
...redeem de...
...is not easy,
...

PETITION! PETITION!! PET

Cut out, paste on a sheet of letter paper, get all the signers ...
September 15th to MRS. GERTRUDE McDOWELL, Fairbury, Neb. ...
one week for work. Read "An Appeal" elsewhere.

WHEREAS, We, the Women of Nebraska, are disfranchised by the Constitution sole...
WHEREAS, We do respectfully demand the right of suffrage—a right which involves ...
ship—which cannot justly be withheld as the following admitted principles of governme...

FIRST—"All men are created equal."
SECOND—"Governments derive their just powers from the cons...
THIRD—"Taxation and representation are inseparable."

Therefore, We, the undersigned Women of Nebraska, earnestly petition the qualifi...
the general election to be held in November, 1882, to vote in favor of the proposed ame...
striking out the word "male."

4

NEBRASKA ELECTION.

The Republican State Ticket Elected by a Handsome Majority.

Laird and Weaver Elected to Congress by 6,000 Each.

Valentine in the Third District in Doubt.

Very Meager Returns from that District.

Female Suffrage Buried Under an Avalanche.

Probably 25,000 Majority Against it.

Scratching on Legislative Tickets was the Rule.

Counting Slow and Many Leading Counties not Heard from.

large population of working men and immigrants.

Fiercely competitive and each eager to claim the victory, the AWSA and the NWSA both converged on Nebraska. In the spring of 1882, the AWSA announced its annual meeting—to be presided over by Erasmus M. Correll—was to be held in Omaha in the fall. Not be outdone, the NWSA announced in early summer that its annual convention would also be held in Omaha at nearly the same time. By August, speakers from Nebraska and around the nation engaged breakneck schedules around the state to raise interest in the respective conventions, which were themselves designed to raise interest in the forthcoming amendment.[44] There was much work to be done. As the *Western Woman's Journal* explained, "Let the watchword from now until the last vote is cast at six o'clock in the afternoon of November 7th, be with every man and woman,—every impartial suffragist, 'work' . . . . Upon every friend of the cause rests a heavy responsibility, that of doing his or her share of the work. . . . Before this responsibility and this duty, every frivolous demand of society, fashion or amusement ought to fall. *Now is the time for work.*"[45]

Under the presidency of Erasmus Correll, the AWSA met in Omaha September 12, 13, and 14. Correll's presidential address noted the gravity of the movement in Nebraska, "a State, we most earnestly hope, that will

be first to adopt an amendment removing the political discrimination against sex, and thereby carry into perfect realization the principles of the Declaration of American Independence, establishing upon a basis of eternal equity a *true* republic."[46] His presidential address was followed by an inspirational speech from Boston suffragist Lucy Stone, who praised the work of Nebraska by saying, "When our feet touched Nebraska soil we felt as though we should take off our shoes, for the place on which we stand was holy ground. Not because of her grand prairies, her magnificent harvests or her giant, limitless boundaries, which we do not have in Massachusetts, but because her men are so noble and progressive that they have offered their wives and mothers and sisters equal rights with themselves."[47] Stone's address was followed by speeches by Henry Blackwell; Nebraskan Orpha Dinsmoor; and the outgoing Governor of Wyoming Territory, John W. Hoyt, who spoke on the success of women's use of the franchise there. Later speeches were given by luminaries of the AWSA, including Amelia Bloomer, who spoke both at length about the history of suffrage initiatives in Nebraska, and paid tribute to the work of Correll, Brooks, Bittenbender, and Colby.

Great attention, however, was paid to the speech given by guest lecturer Susan B. Anthony, who remarked, "This is the third campaign in which my friend Lucy Stone and myself have shared. In three different states—Michigan, Kansas, and Colorado—has the question of woman suffrage been placed before the voters. Though it failed in each state, yet the time is fast approaching when the question will meet success in all these states. . . . Nebraska must not throw away her chance to be the *first* State to adopt woman suffrage. . . . Why should not Nebraska be first in suffrage, as she is ahead on nearly every other national issue?"[48]

Two weeks later, the NWSA held its annual convention in Omaha on September 26, 27, and 28. Because president Elizabeth Cady Stanton was not able to be present, the convention was overseen by acting president Susan B. Anthony. Similar to the AWSA, the NWSA featured speeches by national luminaries and delegates from state associations such as Marietta Bones of Dakota Territory, "who was able to wring tears from the audience by recounting her own unfortunate

Opposite Page:

Center Bottom, Top Background: The suffrage forces gathered petitions to urge the "qualified electors of the state" (men) to support the suffrage amendment. From the Woman Suffrage supplement to *The Western Woman's Journal* (1882), HN Filmstrip Roll 36

Bottom Left: *"The Suffragists."* *Omaha Daily Bee*, Sept. 28, 1882.

Bottom Right: On Nov. 8, 1882, the Lincoln *Daily State Journal* announced state election results, including the resounding defeat of the woman suffrage amendment.

Center Background: After the failure of the 1882 Nebraska suffrage initiative, Clara Bewick Colby edited and published the *Woman's Tribune* (1883-1909), which was the second woman suffrage paper in Nebraska and the second-longest running woman suffrage paper in the United States. HN RG1073AM 54.F21

experiences with a cruel husband whose brutalities drove her to flee with her two children—children whom the courts then ordered her to hand over to her husband."[49]

The tone of the NWSA convention carried more sentimental and sensational appeals than that of the AWSA, and openly engaged the issue of opposition from African-Americans, immigrants, and religiously conservative voters. Anthony spoke at length about the viability of Nebraska's white, middle-class, temperance-focused voters, who unlike Colorado's voters, were seen as more likely to vote for the amendment. She explained Colorado's suffrage defeat, arguing, "Native born-white men, temperance men, liberal-minded decent men voted for it. Against it were the rank and file of Mexicans in southern Colorado, miners, foreigners, German, Irish. The Negro also voted against it. Another class was that imbued with the bigotry and superstition of the past, who believed if the right were given her, that St. Paul would have greatly erred."[50] These remarks were followed by others similar in tone, including those by Missourian Virginia Minor who urged the men of Nebraska "to stand before the world and prove that they had been educated up to the point where they were willing to give women an equal political status with themselves and not assign to her a position inferior to that enjoyed by the Chinese coolie."[51] Certainly, racist and nativist arguments are well known among historians of woman suffrage who have examined their use in urging supporters to vote for suffrage based on expediency.[52] It is interesting, however, to note the example and how these claims were constructed by national suffrage activists in Nebraska.

As Election Day drew near, Harriet R. Shattuck, who had been canvassing the state on behalf of the amendment for the NWSA, worried that "while the advocates are earnestly at work, the opponents are not idle." Shattuck explained, "The German Catholic priest at St. Helena commanded his congregation not to go to the hall to hear the lecture" in support of the amendment. Liquor dealers and patrons opposed the amendment, wrote Shattuck, because "they know too well that their worthless candidates and their bad measures will be less sure of success when women vote." And, she explained further, "There are the men who have made up their minds that women belong at home, and who cannot realize that the

women themselves have a right to choose their 'sphere,' whether it be the home or the profession or the trades. Where they obtained the right to prescribe our sphere they cannot tell, though they claim they have obtained it somehow." Finally, she observed, "There are those who conscientiously fear that women will be changed beings, and that homes will be no longer homes when their wives and daughters are free."[53] Colby also noted the determination of liquor interests to defeat the amendment, and described how "The organ of the Brewers' Association sent out its orders to every saloon, bills posted in conspicuous places by friends of the amendment mysteriously disappeared, or were covered by others of an opposite character, and the greatest pains was [sic] taken to excite the antagonism of foreigners by representing to them that woman suffrage meant prohibition."[54] It was beginning to seem that a campaign that had begun in all earnestness had failed to account for the depth of feeling—and funding—of the opposition.

Was success slipping from their grasp? Writing to *The Woman's Journal* on November 5, Erasmus Correll noted: "Just on the eve of the battle I feel intensely anxious. Day after to-morrow, all over the state, will be, I think, the most important contest for the progress of humanity ever bloodlessly fought. One great element of solicitude is the uncertainty. In ordinary political campaigns, we can form tolerably close approximations in foretelling the results. . . . In this we are entirely at sea. Just in the last moment, the liquor (German) interests are flooding the state with circular letters and tracts against it. . . . I doubt our getting a majority of all the votes cast, although we may."[55]

————

When the morning of November 7, 1882—election day—arrived, Colby described it as ripe with promise:

The morning dawned bright and clear. . . . Everything wore a holiday appearance. Polling places were gaily decorated; banners floated to the breeze, bearing suggestive mottoes: "Are Women Citizens?" "Taxation Without Representation is Tyranny!" "Governments Derive their Just Powers from the Consent of the Governed," "Equality before the Law," etc., etc. Under pavilions, or in adjoining rooms, or in the very shadow of the ballot-box, women presided at well-filled tables, serving refreshments to the voters, and handing to those who would take them, tickets bearing the words: "For Constitutional Amendment Relating to Right of Suffrage," while the national colors floated alike over governing and governed; alike over women working and pleading for their rights as citizens, and men who were selling woman's birth-right for a glass of beer or a vote. It looked like a holiday picnic—the well-dressed people, the flowers, the badges, and the flags.[56]

However, she wrote, "The tragic events of that day would fill a volume," for "the conservative joined hands with the vicious, the egotist with the ignorant, the demagogue with the venial, and when the sun set, Nebraska's opportunity to do the act of simple justice was gone."[57]

The amendment was defeated 50,693 to 25,756.[58] Yet even after its conclusion, emotions continued to run high. Following the election, students at the University of Nebraska enacted a mock funeral complete with an effigy of Susan B. Anthony carried by pallbearers in a coffin, led by a torchlight funeral procession. The students were ultimately thwarted by "another crowd of students who, to preserve the honor of the university, overpowered them and took the effigy away."[59]

Why the resounding defeat? On the one hand, both the Republican and the Democratic parties refused to take a stand on suffrage, and a similar lack of endorsement was found among many candidates. As Colby explained, it had been hoped that the Republicans, at least, would endorse suffrage as a plank in their party platform during their fall convention; however, they did not, and "while individually friendly, they almost to a man avoided the subject."[60] As a result, suffragists were left virtually alone on the political landscape, leaving them vulnerable to a well-organized and well-funded opposition that fostered rampant election fraud, including illegally printed ballots,

misread and misfiled ballots, ballot stuffing, and illegal interference. Shattuck observed, "The liquor interest has been universally represented at the polls by workers against suffrage, and much money has been used by them and by others in the effort to carry the election against us."[61] Addison Sheldon, historian of Nebraska, concurs: "The liquor element felt that giving women the ballot would make it more difficult for it to control elections."[62] Colby lamented, "It will always remain an open question whether the amendment did not, after all, receive an actual majority of all votes cast upon that question."[63]

While all who had worked so hard for the amendment were sorely disappointed, some were also in debt. Correll had taken out a large mortgage to fund his work,[64] and the NWSA reported it "had invested over $5,000 in the Nebraska campaign and was now $500 in debt."[65] Anthony, who had earlier expressed skepticism to Correll about striking out in Nebraska, was angered by this most recent failure and announced at a post-election meeting on November 8 in Omaha that "she had enough of soliciting votes for the cause," and that she would focus her efforts solely on attaining a sixteenth amendment to the federal constitution.[66] Anthony further believed that "while a vast amount of work had been done in Nebraska by her co-laborers, the work was so vast that the hem of the garment of the vast state had yet scarcely been touched. It was totally impossible to canvass every town and neighborhood, and they never would again attempt it." In closing, Anthony "pled with the voters of Nebraska never to submit the question of woman suffrage to the popular vote again."[67]

The early suffrage initiatives mounted in Nebraska reveal the state's important role in establishing some of the first serious state legislative efforts for woman suffrage, and the 1881-1882 campaign reveals Nebraska's vitally important role in positioning the later work of national suffrage activists. Notably, it marked the point where Susan B. Anthony rejected work at the state level to focus instead on working for a federal constitutional amendment, thus marking a dramatic turning point in Anthony's philosophical approach to woman suffrage— popular voters, in her opinion, were no longer to be trusted with such an important decision. And while she would again be seduced by state campaigns in South Dakota and elsewhere, she would devote most of her energy to passing an amendment to the United States Constitution. But as a key moment in the genealogy of national suffrage history, Nebraska's suffrage story should be less about its failure to achieve voting rights for women and more about the opportunities and conflicts it exposed as suffragists strategized the best way to enfranchise women. It exposed the power of the liquor industry's ability to mount a well-organized campaign that uncovered a clash of values that pitted progressives and labor against each another. However, it also exposed the importance of organizing from the grassroots upward, and demonstrated the gains that were to be had by engaging a sophisticated strategy of local organization supported by newspapers, lectures, and conventions that allowed a diverse group of citizens to follow and engage the debate.

As a result of Nebraska's failure to pass a state constitutional amendment supporting woman suffrage, Correll's *Western Woman's Journal* folded in the fall of 1882. Harriet Brooks, perhaps out of frustration, retired from suffrage work, and turned to "the congenial study of sociology."[68] She died in 1888 after a long illness.[69] Erasmus Correll also left suffrage work and in 1890 became editor of the *Ogden Daily Commercial* in Utah. He returned to Nebraska in 1892 and continued his work as an influential newspaperman and politician, and died in 1895 at age 49.[70] Clara Bewick Colby continued her suffrage activism in Nebraska and nationally through her work on the woman's rights newspaper the *Woman's Tribune*, which she published from 1883 to 1909. But in 1916, Colby died without the suffrage for which she had fought so long.[71] Ada M. Bittenbender turned her attention to her work in the law; she later became a prominent attorney for the WCTU, and argued cases for that organization before the Supreme Court of the United States. She died in 1925, the only member of the group of early Nebraska activists to see woman suffrage achieved.[72]

The agitation that led to the suffrage campaign of 1881-1882 never again regained its focused momentum and national support, and although various bills in support of woman suffrage were introduced into the Nebraska legislature nearly every session, none were successful. However, when the United States Congress passed the Nineteenth Amendment, Nebraska suffragists saw their long-sought cause justified when on August 2, 1919, Nebraska became the fourteenth state to ratify the "Anthony Amendment."[73] After the Amendment's final ratification by Tennessee on August 18, 1920, all women of the United States shared the privilege of voting in presidential elections.

————

A verison of this article appeared in the Summer 2009 issue of Nebraska History. *Kristin Mapel Bloomberg is Professor of Women's Studies, Hamline University Endowed Chair in the Humanities, St. Paul, Minnesota.*

Greetings from Plainview Nebr.

THE FLAG SERIES

"Suffragette" postcard, ca. 1910. History Nebraska 11055-2936

Carry Nation Debates Woman Suffrage in Seward
by Patricia C. Gaster

Carry A. Nation's anti-saloon activities in Nebraska in December 1901 and early 1902 took her not only to Lincoln and Omaha but to a number of smaller towns, where she was a star attraction.[1]

In Humboldt, reported the *Valentine Democrat* on January 2, 1902, "A large crowd of people was on the streets all day, eager to get a glimpse of the joint smasher." Her appearance three months later in Valentine prompted the *Democrat* to report on April 3, "There were not seats enough to go 'round and many were compelled to stand."

Nation's visit to Fremont was reported in the *Hastings Tribune* of March 14, 1902, under the headline "Joint Smashing Justified." While in Hastings she spoke at the Kerr Opera House and toured local saloons, where she reportedly disapproved of barroom art as well as liquor. Most of her public presentations attacked saloons and those who patronized them, but at least one of her debates—in Seward on April 15, 1902—was on woman suffrage. Seward's *Blue Valley Blade* on April 16 reported the results of the contest between Mrs. Nation and Judge C. E. Holland of Seward:

"The debate on the suffrage question at the opera house last evening . . . drew out a large and appreciative audience. Mrs. Nation is a motherly looking woman of middle age, and while not a ready debater, announced that she was in the fight for blood and declared it 'no foolin' for her. She opened the debate and for 45 minutes quoted from the [B]ible to sustain her position. She seems to have a very poor opinion of the stronger sex.

"Judge Holland answered, taking the position that women are men's superiors and to give them the ballot would bring them on the same level with men, and thereby spoil all the sanctity and sweetness of the home. Here the Judge paid a most beautiful tribute to women, and said 'It is love that makes life worth the living.'" Judge Holland was armed with typed quotations from the Bible to support his position but his female opponent "used [them]

against him in the last round. The Judge was the acme of courtesy towards his opponent, but gave her many a sharp thrust. Mrs. Nation contends that men are to blame for all the evil in the land and that things will not go right until women are allowed to vote.

"M. D. Carey was chairman and wielded the hatchet for a gavel. Mrs. Nation in her windup gave the judge what she called a 'dressing down,' which evoked shouts of laughter from the audience. He gracefully took his medicine.

"At the close Mrs. Nation asked those who thought that the Judge had won the debate to rise to their feet, but not one in the vast audience thought that way, and then she asked all those who thought that she had won the day should stand up, but only a few arose. So the great question is still unsettled in the minds of the people."

————

Patricia C. Gaster was a longtime assistant editor of Nebraska History, *retiring at the end of 2014. This article first appeared as a "Nebraska Timeline" column distributed to newspapers in October 2011.*

While Carry Nation was perhaps the most notorious link between the suffrage and prohibition movements, she was far from the only one. The close ties between these two movements were an important factor in the anti-suffrage campaign, as the following article demonstrates.

SOUR MILK BISCUIT.

CARRIE NATION

Left: A few weeks after debating suffrage in Seward, Nebraska, Carry Nation addressed a crowd in Ann Arbor, Michigan, on May 3, 1902. Wikimedia Commons

Right: Bain News Service photo. Library of Congress

Thou Shalt Not Vote: Anti-Suffrage in Nebraska, 1914-1920
by Laura McKee Hickman

World War I, the state's electorate rejected proposed suffrage amendments to the constitution three times: following the 1871 constitutional convention, in 1882, and in 1914. In 1917 a limited suffrage act passed the state legislature, but it was nullified by a referendum petition drive until 1919, when the state supreme court declared the petitions fraudulent. Nebraska women did not win full suffrage until 1920, when the national amendment was ratified.[1]

Why was Nebraska one of the last states west of the Mississippi to grant the ballot to women? The answer requires an examination both of Nebraska's electorate and its organized anti-suffrage movement. As the possibility of woman suffrage became more real in the 1910s, those individuals who felt most threatened organized against the suffragists and used every force at their disposal to stop the extension of the franchise; ironically, many of them were women.

Suffrage failed to pass in Nebraska for many reasons, but most important was that a large segment of the all-male voting population opposed it. Opposition was strongest among certain religious and ethnic groups whose cultural perspective and religious teachings formed shared values. This trend can be seen in the nineteenth and early twentieth centuries, when party affiliation was heavily defined by religious or ethnic factors. The values embraced by the Democratic Party included laissez-faire economics, personal liberty, and social conservatism. The party platform, therefore, consistently rejected prohibition, tariffs, and woman suffrage. In Nebraska, the Democratic coalition com bined Catholics, German Lutherans, and other ritualistic religions, Southern migrants, and many of the wealthiest segments of the population.[2] These groups made up much of Nebraska's anti-suffrage vote.

Nationally, immigrant religious groups also tended to be affiliated with the Democrats, the party of personal liberty. About 55 percent of German Lutherans and members of the German Reformed Church, both ritualistic religions, joined the Democratic Party. Native religious

One hundred fifty years has passed since the Seneca Falls Convention, the event that marks the opening of the woman's suffrage movement in the United States. Our understanding of that movement, however, remains clouded by missing pieces and unexplored biases. In particular, opposition to woman suffrage has only begun to be explored. Although all of Nebraska's neighbors to the west, north, and south passed full woman suffrage before

Left: State Senator John Mattes of Nebraska City owned Mattes Brewery and led the senate's German-American coalition. HN RG2141-1445

groups—Baptists, Methodists, Congregationalists, and Presbyterians—tended to be more pietistic and voted overwhelmingly Republican, the party of purification, politically and morally. In turn-of-the-century Nebraska, these native religious groups made up only about 36 percent of the state's population.[3] Nebraska's strong immigrant vote, as well as the ritualistic religions that many immigrants practiced, helps explain the failure of woman suffrage in the late nineteenth century.

The religious group most cohesive in its rejection of woman suffrage and most overwhelmingly Democratic despite ethnic variables, was the Roman Catholic Church. Whether of Irish, Polish, French, Dutch, Bohemian, or German background, Catholics voted Democratic in huge percentages. In 1906 more than 29 percent of all Nebraskans claimed affiliation with the Catholic Church, by far the largest single denomination in the state.[4]

The German Catholics were the most conservative. In response to progressive era reforms, the German-American *Central-Verein*, a national organization, formed a union to reform society in its conservative mold. The union pledged to work against those Catholics calling for greater Americanization of the church. According to historian Philip Gleason, "German Catholics in particular were convinced that the surest bulwark to the immigrant's religion was the maintenance of his traditional cultural heritage against the forces of Americanization.[5] The *Central-Verein*'s greatest concerns included the secularization of American society and the separation of church and state, but the maintenance of the traditional culture would lead German Catholics to fight to include their language in public school instruction, to battle against prohibitionists, and to maintain the traditional family structure.

Like many other Germans in the United States, Nebraska Germans saw in reform movements such as prohibition and woman suffrage the tools to destroy their traditional culture. The assumption was that, if women were given the vote, many of them would be inclined to support prohibition. Furthermore, woman suffrage was seen as a threat to German family values, as well as demoralizing to women who would no longer be sheltered in the home. In the 1882 vote for a woman suffrage amendment, precincts with a German population greater than 50 percent reject-

ed the amendment by ten to one. Overall, the amendment failed by only two to one.[6]

Whether Catholic or not, in Nebraska Germans formed the largest non-English ethnic group. Germans made up nearly 54 percent of the state's foreign-born population, and more than 23 percent of the total population in 1910.[7] Furthermore, the German community, prior to World War I, was very strong socially and politically. German newspapers had a huge circulation (there were fourteen in Nebraska and forty in the nation), many grade schools taught the language, and the German-American Alliance provided a political organization. This organization was key in preventing the passage of prohibition in Nebraska for many years.[8] The dual issues of woman suffrage and prohibition further developed the Germans' self-consciousness as a minority group because the group's cohesiveness in votes on these issues, just as later attacks on the German language, united the German community.

The movement to prohibit alcohol had a long history in the state. Advocates of prohibition argued that its passage would create "a social order universally congenial to entrepreneurial capitalism."[9] During the vote on Nebraska's 1871 constitution, a prohibition amendment received 37 percent approval. By 1874 a Prohibition Party had formed and offered candidates for governor and other offices. Prohibition sentiments grew steadily toward the turn of the century. But prohibition's growing popularity also caused increased controversy and threatened to split Nebraska's major political parties.[10]

Many other immigrants, along with Germans, saw prohibition as an attack on their culture and woman suffrage as the weapon. The National Brewers' Association, along with many others, including prohibitionists, believed that giving, women the vote would result in prohibition. The brewers quietly spent large amounts of money advertising against the extension of the franchise.[11] The association saw "the unreasoning interference of women" as the largest obstacle to "rational temperance reform."[12] Even after the 1917 implementation of state wide prohibition in Nebraska, many continued to see the breweries' involvement in anti-suffrage campaigns as a "last ditch effort to repeal prohibition."[13]

Suffrage thus failed in Nebraska prior to 1914 due to

the anti-suffrage sentiments of the state's all-male voting population. While many emigrant groups, brewers, and Catholics could be counted on to oppose prohibition, no organized anti-suffrage movement existed in the state until 1914, when the Nebraska Woman Suffrage Association launched an initiative campaign to place the issue on the ballot.

The suffrage movement, unlike any other civil rights movement in history, was not merely a struggle between the powerful and the powerless. It was not a struggle between men and women. Nor was it a class struggle. The leadership of the anti-suffragists and pro-suffragists shared the same social class, and neither group encouraged participation by non-whites or non-Christians. The leadership of both organizations tended to be college educated, white, middle to upper class, and socially active.

The woman suffrage counter movement has often been distorted by studies relying solely on the perspective of the suffragists. Women opposed to suffrage have been portrayed as mere puppets of the powerful brewery and industrial interests, or as society matrons unaware of the difficulties faced by poor women. More recent studies of the anti-suffragists have revealed that the men's organizations were mere subsidiaries to the women's organizations, and the female leadership, very much aware of the life faced by poor women, simply disagreed that the vote was the means of achieving change.[14]

The fallacy that women opposed to woman suffrage were society butterflies, with no real concept of the hardships faced by less fortunate women, has been exposed as suffrage rhetoric, or misconception. In fact, female opponents of suffrage embraced the twentieth century idea of womanhood—the extension of women into the public realm—almost to the same degree as did their sisters fighting for the ballot. The major difference between the two groups of women was the extent to which they believed women could effectively contribute in the political realm. The anti-suffragists believed the ballot would only hamper women's unique contributions to society.[15]

The longest-lived anti-suffrage organization, the Massachusetts Association Opposed to the Further Extension of Suffrage to Women, listed the many philanthropic, charitable, educational, and civic activities of its female

members.[16] While nineteenth century anti-suffrage spokeswomen Catherine Beecher and Sara Josephina Hale had argued that women's sphere was entirely domestic, twentieth century anti-suffragists had moved beyond the Victorian era concepts of home and hearth and accepted the idea of progressive activism for women. Josephine Dodge, founder of the National Association Opposed to Woman Suffrage, worked many years with the Legal Aid Society and the National Federation of Day Nurseries. Very much aware of the plight of poor women, she encouraged her membership to continue work in social reform and charity, and discouraged a total focus on home. The General Federation of Women's Clubs, by far the most socially active group of women in the nation, refused to endorse woman suffrage for many years. Like the anti-suffragists in general, many club women feared having the ballot would only hamper their work.[17]

The leadership of Nebraska's anti-suffragists shared the civic-mindedness of the national associations. When America entered World War I in 1917, many of the women went to work. Mrs. William A. Smith of Omaha, secretary of the Nebraska Association Opposed to Woman Suffrage, became chairman of the National League for Women's Services, "a non-partisan, non-political war organization."[18] The anti-suffragists believed that once women became politicized, their ability to reform society would be impaired because they would no longer be disinterested parties. "Women in politics would destroy

---

Opposite Page

Background: *The Omaha Bee* of July 26, 1914, profiled prominent local women on both sides of the suffrage issue. The leadership of the anti-suffragists and pro-suffragists shared the same social class, and neither group encouraged participation by non-whites or non-Christians.

Bottom Right: Cathloic handbill. HN RG1073

Bottom Left: Anti-Suffrage pamphlets published by the Omaha-based Nebraska Association Opposed to Woman Suffrage. Suffragists Katherine Sumney and Grace Richardson (see p. 64) preserved these and others in a set of scrapbooks later donated to History Nebraska. HN RG1073.AM

Top Right: "Ten Reason Why..." Paper flyer. HN RG1073

charity." Many female anti-suffragists believed that their social contributions benefited society as much as, if not more than, men's political work. The ballot, by placing greater responsibilities on women and by changing their role as neutral, non-political beings, would compromise their unique contributions to society.[19]

Furthermore, anti-suffragists argued that the suffragists' lack of civic spirit and selfishness made it "easier to believe in the fallacy that the vote will change all the evils of the world, than it is to give hours [of] ... unheralded work toward the amelioration of the conditions of women, children, and the unfortunate." Anti-suffragists proved their point by comparing philanthropic statistics in eastern states, where there was no female suffrage, and western states with female suffrage. They concluded the suffragists were "anti-female, anti-family, and anti-American."[20]

It was these sentiments, along with the 1914 suffrage initiative, that led to the creation of formal anti-suffrage organizations in Nebraska. During the campaign, Josephine Dodge, president of the National Association Opposed to Woman Suffrage, traveled to Omaha along with other noted personalities to speak against the issue. Mrs. J. W. Crumpacker, an anti-suffragist from Kansas, joined Dodge and two veteran campaigners sent by the Massachusetts anti-suffrage association to fight the amendment in a campaign the Woman's Protest claimed was funded by the Nebraska Men's League Opposed to Woman Suffrage. Out-of-state anti-suffrage associations, despite sending these few relatively unknown campaigners, were not particularly worried about the outcome of the vote. Nebraska, like other states with large German populations, could be relied on to reject suffrage, which it did. Also working in favor of the anti-suffragists was the confrontational and controversial personality of the National Woman Suffrage Association president, Anna Howard Shaw. During her visit to Omaha during the 1914 campaign, Shaw verbally attacked a state judge who refused to allow Nebraska women to vote for the office of superintendent, though women could vote for school board members. The anti-suffragists widely publicized the event: "Here is a woman from an eastern state who knows nothing about Nebraska statutes, refuting in positive language the opinion of a man who has spent years in the practice of the law."[21]

With the help of more experienced organizers, a meeting was held at the home of Mrs. E. P. Peck in Omaha and the Nebraska Association Opposed to Woman Suffrage was founded. Peck, after a brief period as chairwoman of the executive committee, became president of the association in September 1914; Mrs. L. F. Crofoot was named chair woman of the executive committee; the secretary was Mrs. William Archibald Smith, and the treasurer was Mrs. Charles C. George. Other board members included Mrs. N. P. Dodge, Jr., Mrs. R. T. Hamilton, Mrs. C. S. Elgutter, Mrs. T. J. Mackaye, Mrs. C. F. McGrew, Mrs. C. Peters, Mrs. John H. Butler, and Miss Jessie Millard. Like anti-suffrage associations in other states, the Nebraska association was staffed and run by women, and its membership was overwhelmingly female. As in the national and other state associations, the role of men in the Nebraska Association Opposed to Woman Suffrage was marginal.[22]

Throughout the state, but especially in the largest cities of Omaha and Lincoln, the anti-suffragists recruited, organized, and raised funds through teas, luncheons, balls at luxurious hotels, and junior auxiliaries at colleges. They set out to educate the public on the evils of suffrage through literature, advertising, public speaking, or even playing dirty on some occasions. The anti-suffragists broke into parades disguised as suffragists to make their opposition look foolish.[23]

The first organized male opposition to the Nebraska suffragists also came from Omaha in 1914. The Nebraska Men's Association Opposed to Woman Suffrage (NMAOWS) published a manifesto in July and August of the 1914 petition campaign for a suffrage amendment. Signed by prominent community leaders, most of whom had wives and daughters leading the Nebraska anti-suffragists, the manifesto carried affidavits by the city's preachers from various denominations. The first publication by the men listed their arguments against the extension of the franchise to women. They began with political arguments: "Franchise is a privilege of government granted only to those to whom the government sees fit to grant it"; it was not a birthright, nor a right connected to taxation. To avoid a complete rejection of the principles of the nation's founders, the authors further claimed woman suffrage was inconsistent with the founding fathers' vision of republican government. Female suffrage was never suggested in the original constitution because the founders feared "an excitable and emotional suffrage" would destroy the republic, a danger the manifesto's authors foresaw in a veiled reference to the fifteenth amendment and the huddled masses fueling the cities' political machines by the overextension of the franchise to "highly questionable" segments of the population. The men's arguments concluded with moral issues. Women did not belong in the political realm because their place was the "realm of sentiment, ... love, ... gentler, kinder and holier attributes, that make the name of wife, mother, and sister next to the name of God himself."[24]

The next month's publication was wholly moral in tone. Adolf Hult, pastor of Immanuel Lutheran, claimed that "Suffragism [is] Gripped by Feminism." Citing radical feminists' views, Reverend Hult claimed that the suffrage movement had been taken over by "lust and immorality." Fearing that the fall of woman meant the fall of the world, Hult asked, "Must men put on the iron glove?" Other arguments were more logical, such as that of Reverend John Williams of St. Barnabas Episcopal Church, who drew a distinction between the mainstream suffragists and the radical fringe. Nonetheless, he argued that the failure of the mainstream suffragists to suppress or refute the radicals was subversive to Christian morality, marriage, and home life. The damaging effect of woman suffrage on home life was a pervasive theme throughout the manifesto. The ministers claimed the Victorian ideal of domesticity had been preordained by God: "God meant for women to reign over home, and most good women reject politics because woman suffrage will destroy society." A minister from Ponca, Nebraska, quoted scripture implying that God simply forgot to list the commandment, women shall not vote.[25]

In response to the suffragists' publication of priests' testimonials favoring suffrage, L. F. Crofoot, a prominent Catholic lawyer among the male anti-suffragists, authored a pamphlet, "Lest Catholic Men Be Misled." He argued that a "good Catholic" would never support the movement because Dr. Anna Howard Shaw, president of the National American Woman Suffrage Association, "spurns all male authority—even St. Paul who she claimed enslaved

Left: "Woman's Rights #2," detail of a 1902 stereograph image by Omaha and Lincoln photographer J.M. Calhoun. One of the arguments against equal suffrage—made both humorously and seriously—was that it would upset traditional gender roles. HN RG3279-2

Bottom Left: Mary Nash Crofoot, president of the Nebraska Association Opposed to Woman Suffrage. Courtesy of Mrs. Michael Crofoot

Bottom Right: Mary's husband, Lodowick F. Crofoot. From *Nebraskans, 1854-1904* (Omaha: Bee Publishing Co., 1904).

women." Nor would a "good Catholic woman" embrace feminism."[26]

The men's anti-suffrage association became the Men's League Opposed to Woman Suffrage by the time of the November 1914 election. Advertising, especially in the Omaha papers, was their main tactic to defeat the suffrage amendment. Their position focused on two major arguments: the passage of woman suffrage would compel women to serve on juries; and, again quoting radical feminists, suffrage was simply the first step for women who demanded "FREEDOM and POWER" in their attempts to change "HOME and MARRIAGE."[27] The Men's League was not the only male group advertising in Omaha's newspapers in 1914. The Massachusetts Men's Association Opposed to Woman Suffrage argued that women's inability to enforce the laws they would help make was objectionable. Nor was it in the interest of the state to more than double the electorate with a segment of the population having so little experience in business.

The men's anti-suffrage associations were much smaller, less well organized, and frequently subordinate to the women's anti-suffrage organizations. Their contributions' to the anti-suffrage movement were important, however, because while many female anti-suffragists were unwilling to take a public stand, the men's organizations could do so. Furthermore, the men's associations provided funding for the campaigns. Nebraska's female anti-suffragists reported that the Men's League "helped with the responsibility" of the 1914 counter-campaign, and provided financial help in later fights."[28]

The National Association Opposed to Woman Suffrage had organized only three years earlier, in 1911. Its leadership was entirely female, and its membership was more than 90 percent female. The state anti-suffrage organizations, like the Nebraska Association Opposed to Woman Suffrage, paid an annual fee to the national body which, in turn, helped support the state level. Local organizations were also formed. For example, Fremont, Lincoln, and Grand Island had very strong local chapters of the anti-suffrage association. The state association in 1914 had a membership of between 1,200 and 1,300, only about 100 of whom were active, dues-paying members. Many of the associate members belonged to groups affiliated with the Nebraska Association Opposed to Woman Suffrage, such as the Men's League and the Wage Earner's League. The Wage Earner's League represented female wage earners such as clerks, secretaries, and teachers. Founded by May McNamara and Alice Gilchrist in 1911, its five hundred members worked with Nebraska anti-suffragists.[29]

Why were so many women opposed to having the franchise? The only reasonable answer must be that they feared the loss of something valuable in return for gaining the ballot. While a few noble souls may have organized to preserve the charity anti-suffragists claimed would be lost if women entered politics, it is much more likely that many were drawn by concern over a loss more personal, a loss in status. Many women clung to the Victorian ideal because they feared the social change that suffrage would bring would also bring a loss of the privileges and protections they had been accorded as the so-called weaker sex. Suffrage, they argued, would cause men to deny dependent women support and would cause a dramatic increase in divorce rates, forcing many women into the labor force. Political responsibilities would overburden already busy women; and the image of the new woman would destroy the respect and status they enjoyed as wives and mothers.

Nationally, the rhetoric of the power struggle waged by the anti-suffragists also portrayed a concern with status. Anti-suffragists tended to support the laissez-faire philosophy of wages, arguing that women were paid less because their labor was worth less. Most believed in the preferential hiring of male breadwinners and the removal of women from industrial work. Female anti-suffragists fought to maintain the status and wealth of the men who protected them by preserving the industrial system. Similarly they opposed unions, reformers, socialists, communists, and anarchists, arguing that suffrage would empower these groups by giving a larger political voice to industrial workers and the foreign-born, and eventually bring an end to democracy and capitalism in the United States. Other arguments foresaw the growing power of the lower classes because "respectable" women's fertility would suffer due to the added burden of suffrage. Eugenics and birth control for race improvement also found a place in the rhetoric of the anti-suffragists.[30]

One compromise was offered to the status-conscious

46

anti-suffragists in 1911. A limited suffrage movement founded in Philadelphia would pass suffrage, but only for educated, or middle to upper class women. Ironically, both camps resoundingly rejected the limited suffrage compromise as narrow-minded, parochial, and undemocratic. Half measures were clearly unacceptable to either side. However, Nebraska legislators may have considered a similar compromise: the exclusion of farm women.[31]

Following the initiative defeat in 1914, Nebraska suffragists resigned themselves to a four-year wait before a new initiative could be proposed. But in 1917 the state legislature surprised both suffragists and anti-suffragists by passing a limited suffrage act allowing women to vote in municipal elections and for presidential electors, the most that could be done without an amendment to the state constitution. The bill had nearly been foiled by the German-American coalition in the senate led by Senator John Mattes of Nebraska City, owner and founder of Mattes' Brewery. In the spring of 1917 two limited suffrage bills were simultaneously proposed in the upper and lower houses of the legislature. The senate version was quickly killed by Mattes as president pro tempore of the senate and chairman of the sifting committee. Poised to repeat the process with the version passed by the house, Mattes's plans were disrupted in April with the U.S. declaration of war on the country of his birth. With his patriotism and culture under attack, not to mention his livelihood with the recent adoption of prohibition, Mattes and the other Germans in the legislature were forced to make a deal. A German language law threatened by repeal became the vehicle to passage of the limited suffrage act. Legislators favoring woman suffrage voted to continue to allow German to be taught in the public schools, and Mattes supported limited suffrage for Nebraska women.[32]

Prohibition had passed in Nebraska almost simultaneously with limited woman suffrage, and with the full support of the Nebraska Woman Suffrage Association. Their 1917 convention adopted a resolution favoring nation-wide prohibition: "Whereas the conserving of all grains... is needed by our allies and vitally necessary to the winning of the war... BE IT RESOLVED, that the Nebraska Womans (sic) Suffrage Association in state convention assembled urges upon the United States Congress... the passage of... prohibition."[33]

The political power of the German-Americans and the Brewers' Association was seriously curtailed when the United States entered World War I. As xenophobia gripped the nation, anything associated with Germany became anathema. Both suffragists and anti-suffragists smeared their opposition with connection to German imports: anti-suffragists were portrayed as mere fronts for the brewery gangs; suffragists were in league with socialists.[34] German-American political power decreased dramatically as their loyalty came under question, and the issues they had fought against for so long gained in popularity. The Democratic Party endorsed both national prohibition and full woman suffrage in the 1918 platform, causing a mass exodus by German-American voters until the 1920s.[35] But there was nowhere else to turn.

Nebraska had fifteen breweries and one distillery in 1917, most of which were in Omaha. That city's mayor, James Dahlman, became the spokesman for the anti-suffragists.[36] Mayor Dahlman was the frontman for the city's political machine run by Tom Dennison and Frank Johnson. Johnson's predecessor, Edward Rosewater, published the Omaha Bee, a paper that tended to oppose women's participation in politics until Rosewater's death in 1906. The nineteenth century machine had depended on alcohol, gambling, and prostitution; female suffrage posed a clear threat to the machine's power. Dahlman, by now termed the "perpetual mayor," considered women as qualified as men to vote, but feared that woman suffrage would usher in prohibition, the only reason, he claimed, that he would vote against the extension of the franchise.[37]

Once the limited woman suffrage law passed Nebraska's legislature, the state's anti-suffrage association organized in full force to block its implementation. The Nebraska Association Opposed to Woman Suffrage voiced the arguments of their national coalition. They appealed to those resistant to social change by evoking established social myths: political competition with men would lead to a loss of modesty and gentleness while forcing women to become more aggressive; suffrage would double divorce rates by causing discord within the home, and would destroy good wives and mothers who would neglect the home; women would merely duplicate their husband's vote because they have no knowledge of government; and because of their physical inferiority, they would be unable to enforce the laws they would help create. Anti-suffragists also appealed to the nativist, racist, and class-based attitudes of early twentieth century society, but so did suffragists.[38]

Nebraska anti-suffragists also appealed to the voters whose mandate against woman suffrage in 1914 had been cast aside by the 1917 legislative act. In a letter to the editor of the *Omaha World-Herald* following the passage of the limited suffrage law, the Nebraska Association Opposed to Woman Suffrage claimed that the suffragists had' harassed and intimidated the state legislature into passing the bill "over the veto of the people. This is the worst blow to representative government that our country has received.... Legislators forget that they represent the people, not the suffragists." Antis further warned "that when a handful of women seek to set aside the verdict of the voters at the polls they make more enemies for their cause than they suspect."[39]

Nebraskans opposed to woman suffrage set out to prove that claim with the referendum petition of 1917. For legal advice the anti-suffragists turned to Senator John F. Moriarty, a leading member of the Democratic Party, and a Catholic. Moriarty drafted the referendum petition circulated by the Nebraska Association Opposed to Woman Suffrage and secured the services of an experienced referendum organizer.[40] In just three months the Nebraska Association Opposed to Woman Suffrage collected more than 30,000 names, blocking the law until it could be voted upon by the male electorate at the next election.

German-Americans were repeatedly blamed for organizing the petition drive.[41] At the height of war hysteria, the use of anti-German rhetoric would play nicely for the suffragists to push the patriotic into the suffrage camp. The *Woman Citizen*, the national organ of the National Woman Suffrage Association, reported that the German American Alliance had publicly stated its involvement in Nebraska's referendum to nullify woman suffrage.[42]

But German-Americans were not the only group opposed to woman suffrage. L. F. Crofoot, a leading anti-suffragist along with his wife, was also president of the Nebraska Prosperity League, a pro-liquor campaign organization. Senator John F. Moriarty, the legislator who helped the anti-suffragists organize their referendum

drive, may have been motivated equally by Catholic conservatism and self-interest. He was the attorney for Omaha's saloonkeepers.

Due to wartime hysteria against the Kaiser and beer, Germans and saloon-keepers could not openly work against woman suffrage, but the Nebraska Association Opposed to Woman Suffrage could. Like the national organization, Nebraska's female anti-suffragists were active in the public domain, but they shied away from political work, even to stop the passage of suffrage. Mrs. William Archibald Smith reported her attitudes about working for the Nebraska anti-suffrage association: "I was elected the first secretary of the organization and I took the work I must say at first rather unwillingly because I did not want to become involved in any political work, ... [But] there was a demand among a large majority of women... that we did not want to enter political life, that there should be an organization which would publicly express our opposition.... [There] was a principle involved."[43] Such attitudes are key to an examination of the failed signature collection process because most of the women refused to carry the petitions themselves. Instead the association paid others to collect signatures, opening the process to fraud.

During the suffragists' 1914 initiative campaign, nearly all petitioners had been female members of the Nebraska Woman Suffrage Association. One anti-suffragist claimed the suffragists did not have to hire help because "they have a great deal more time to spare than we have." The Nebraska anti-suffragists in 1917, however, relied almost completely on hired circulators outside Omaha, where there were nearly no women circulators. One exception was Maud May, who personally took charge of the campaign in Fremont and almost single-handedly secured the quota of signatures for Dodge County. In Omaha, a few women did circulate petitions. Mrs. Charles C. George, treasurer of the Nebraska Association Opposed to Woman Suffrage, claimed she "circulate[d] petitions, not privately at all, but taking them down—for instance in the packing houses" and to several banks and mercantile stores. Most of the circulators, however, were not loyal anti-suffragists, but men who needed to make money.[44]

Nebraska's anti-suffrage movement shared other similarities with the national anti-suffragists. The Nebraska

Association Opposed to Woman Suffrage had connections to moneyed interests. Among the membership of the women's and men's leagues were names associated with big business, particularly in Omaha: president of the electric company, grocers, seven bank presidents, numerous lawyers, the president of the Omaha Gas Company, and railroad and other mass transit company executives. Capitalists and industrialists, along with their wives and daughters, made up the leadership of the Nebraska anti-suffragists.[45] However, the Nebraska Association Opposed to Woman Suffrage categorically denied that the referendum was carried on under the direction or control of any outside organization: "The Nebraska association was wholly responsible for this themselves."[46]

Nor would anti-suffragists admit any connections to the liquor interests. The secretary of the anti-suffrage association claimed, "It is just as unfair to accuse the association of being supported by the saloons and the vice interests as it is to make the suffrage association responsible for such women as Rose Pastor Stokes and Vardaman, and LaFollette's actions.[47] No analysis of the Nebraska petitions for connections to liquor interests was ever attempted, but in Ohio's 1914 campaign suffragists investigated and found that a liquor organization had paid for an anti-suffrage pamphlet that was distributed door-to-door. In North Dakota, a dry state, the referendum attempt failed miserably. In every state suffrage campaign, some link to the liquor interests was charged against the anti-suffrage organizations.[48] Nebraska had been dry only a few months when the referendum was initiated, so "liquor organizations [were still able to] muster considerable strength."[49] Many ex-saloonkeepers and Germans were among the circulators or allied with the anti-suffragists for prohibition reasons according to some Nebraska newspapers.[50] The Nebraska anti-suffragists probably did not seek an alliance with the anti-prohibitionists, but the shared goals would have naturally brought those seeking to legalize alcohol into the anti-suffragists' camp. The same is true of industrialists. Men and women who expected their status and income to decline because of the growing power of women would be more likely to join with the anti-suffragists.

The Nebraska Woman Suffrage Association demanded to review the referendum petition signatures, first as a threat to publish the names of the signers. They soon found such tactics unnecessary. Many of the signatures were in alphabetical order and appeared to be forgeries. Preliminary investigation found evidence of extensive fraud, including improper collection of signatures, the names of minor and deceased signers, and addresses that did not exist.[51] The state supreme court nullified the referendum petition effort in 1919, restoring limited suffrage for women until the national amendment passed the next year. Due to widespread charges of fraud in the referendum campaign, Nebraska's anti-suffragists failed to prove that Nebraskans opposed the expansion of the electorate.

It remains unclear whether the voters would have overturned the legislature's limited suffrage bill. Anti-suffragists, if not a majority, were certainly a very strong minority. They were not, however, a monolith. Anti-suffragists were divided on many issues: some opposed woman suffrage because it would strengthen prohibitionists, others rejected the massive social change they perceived to be part of the suffrage agenda, and many women feared the ballot because they would lose social deference without gaining political equality. Taken as a whole, those opposed to woman suffrage made a powerful force in Nebraska, but their efforts became moot with the ratification of the nineteenth amendment in 1920.

———————

This article appeared in the Summer 1999 issue of Nebraska History. *At the time, the author chaired the history department at Duchesne Academy of the Sacred Heart in Omaha. Dr. Hickman has served as Duchesne's principal since 2002.*

Heckling President Wilson: Omaha Suffragist Rheta Childe Dorr
by Eileen Wirth

The scene was the East Room of the White House on June 30, 1914, a day so hot that the tar of the pavement buckled. A delegation of five hundred upper-class members of the General Federation of Women's Clubs clad in suffragist white dresses crowded in to present President Woodrow Wilson with their resolution demanding suffrage. Their leader was Omaha native Rheta Childe Dorr, who forthrightly addressed the president:

"As practical women, we know that in this Congress, controlled by the Chief Executive, the suffrage amendment is entirely in your hands," she said.[1]

This was not the polite exchange that Wilson had evidently expected when he invited these genteel social leaders into the White House. But now the Congressional Union for Woman Suffrage seized the opportunity to make front page national news by confronting the president in his own house, with the formidable Dorr in the starring role.[2]

An Omaha doctor's rebellious daughter, the forty-seven-year-old Dorr had been preparing for such a moment all her life, and chronicled it in her autobiography.

As a child, when Dorr heard someone ask if parents were disappointed by the birth of a daughter, she would jump up and down and holler "Lil girls just as good as lil boys." At age twelve, she sneaked out of her house to attend an Omaha suffrage rally featuring Susan B. Anthony and Elizabeth Cady Stanton. Her parents learned that she had joined National Woman Suffrage Association by reading her name in the paper the next day.[3]

Dorr moved to Lincoln with her family and attended the University of Nebraska in 1884-85 but hated it, and dropped out after reading Henrik Ibsen's *A Doll's House*—a play about a woman trapped in a stifling marriage—in a literature class. She then horrified her family by getting a job at the Lincoln Post Office, where she formed a social conscience by encountering immigrants from around the world.[4] In 1890, she left Lincoln for art school in New York and only returned to Nebraska for short visits. She continued to rebel against restrictions on women.

Dorr got married and had a son but divorced her husband because he wouldn't allow her sufficient independence. In New York she became a newspaper society editor who helped broker an alliance between immigrant working women and wealthy club women.[5] She also traveled to Europe to study its suffrage movements and did ghostwriting for Britain's most militant suffragist, Emmeline Pankhurst.[6] Returning to the US, Dorr served in 1913-14 as the first editor of *The Suffragist*, the official organ of the Congressional Union for Woman Suffrage, a new organization founded by Alice Paul and Lucy Burns.[7] Inspired by the British suffragette movement, the Congressional Union emerged at a time when suffrage leaders decided to take advantage of a changing political climate to push for a federal suffrage amendment instead of seeking the vote state by state.

The election of 1912 had brought Wilson to power, and Democrats also controlled both houses of Congress for the first time in years. Wilson did not support woman suffrage, but suffragist leaders believed that inducing him to change his stance was the key to getting Congress to send the proposed amendment to the states for ratification.

"Over these (congressional) majorities, President Wilson exercised despotic power. All we had to do was induce President Wilson to instruct Congress to pass the amendment. The whole suffrage question thus reduced itself to winning one casting vote, that of Woodrow Wilson… that was by making President Wilson see that without it the Democratic Party could not long retain power," because more states were enfranchising women.[8]

Dorr and other suffrage leaders "decided on a session with the President which would make him appear before the country as an opponent, not only on legislation on which his party had not spoken, but specifically as an opponent of woman suffrage."[9]

According to Dorr, Wilson liked and respected women "as long as they were domestic and ornamental. In any other role, he simply ignored them."[10] Dorr would not be ignored, but felt the pressure of the occasion.

The Confrontation

When Dorr marched into the White House, the five hundred women "crowded against my body so closely that streams of perspiration drenched me and I felt like an animal in a cage."[11] Soon after, Wilson's aide Joseph Tumulty arrived and told the club women that after they presented their resolution and spoke to the president, he would address them. Then the women would form a line and Wilson would shake their hands. "The President especially desires to shake every one of you by the hand," he said.[12]

Left: Rheta Childe Dorr, 1913, the year she began editing *The Suffragist*. Library of Congress

Center: A woman sells copies of *The Suffragist* in 1914. Library of Congress

Right: President Woodrow Wilson long opposed a constitutional amendment to guarantee women the vote. He said it was a matter for the states. Library of Congress

Top: Members of the National Women's Party picket President Wilson in Chicago on October 20, 1916. After years of protests, Wilson eventually relented and voiced support for the Nineteenth Amendment. Library of Congress

According to an account in *the New York Times* the next day, the meeting "which was otherwise of a friendly and informal sort was marred at its close by a painful misunderstanding." Dorr and two other suffrage leaders, Mrs. Harvey Wiley and Mrs. Ellis Logan, had made speeches then Wiley and Dorr debated with Wilson about his views on suffrage.[13] As Dorr recalled it, she raised the issue of what the Democratic platform contained.

"Mr. President, the last time we came to you on this business, you told us that you were firmly determined never to inaugurate or put through any important piece of legislation which was not expressly provided for in the Baltimore (Democratic Party) platform. Since then, however, you have not only put through an important piece of legislation which was not provided for in the Baltimore Platform, but one which was expressly provided against in the Baltimore Platform and on which you went to the country."[14]

At this, Dorr recalled, Wilson turned so visibly cold that the women behind Dorr "actually swayed in alarm, pressing closer to my streaming back."[15] Dorr, however, was undeterred.

"Mr. President, you said you did this thing because changed conditions warranted changed policies. We agree with you, and we are here to tell you how importantly the whole woman suffrage situation has changed since the Baltimore Platform was written, and how changed action on your part is called for." Dorr reminded Wilson that in 1914, 3.6 million women voted in nine states instead of four in 1912 when he was elected. She also told him that no future presidential candidate could run while the suffrage amendment was stuck in Congress.[16]

"I made it perfectly clear that the amendment was held up by his deliberate intention, and I said: 'Mr. President, all this being true, we ask you to act immediately and we ask your assurance now that you will so act.?'"[17]

Wilson responded that Dorr knew that constitutionally, each state determined suffrage; he refused to interfere with this process. He told the women that he would "never countenance any change in the electorate except through state action."[18] Dorr was not persuaded.

"If that is the case, Mr. President, would you kindly tell us why you actively approved the amendment to the Constitution providing for the direct election of the United States Senators?"[19] When Wilson told the women that he had no power over amendments, Dorr responded with a reminder of political realities.

"As practical women, we know that in this Congress, controlled by the Chief Executive, the suffrage amendment is entirely in your hands." The women were simply seeking his help in getting Congress to send the amendment to the states for ratification.[20]

Some of the president's entourage seemed amused as Dorr presented her arguments. Wilson was not.

"I think that it is not proper for me to stand here and be cross-examined by you," he said. He turned and left the room "forgetting all about shaking hands."[21]

In the *New York Times* account, the discussion ended more graciously. Dorr thanked Wilson for his courtesy and Wilson responded that "it has been a pleasant occasion" before he withdrew. However, a deck headline on the story told readers that "Some Women Didn't Hear President's Friendly Parting Words with Leaders and Started to Hiss."[22]

The Aftermath

Although some club women feared that Dorr had unwisely antagonized the president, she was not concerned. As she predicted, the story was front page news across the country the next day.[23] There was some adverse public reaction to the incident, including from suffragists.

In a letter to Wilson published in the *New York Times*, Dr. Anna Howard Shaw, president of the National Woman Suffrage Association, said that no representative of her group had been present. She also stated that "We greatly deplore any act in the name of woman suffrage which mars the record of dignity, lawfulness and patriotism which has marked the conduct of the campaign to obtain political justice for women in the United States."[24]

The *Times* went on to warn that the Congressional Union approach fed speculation "about what effect, if any, women's entrance into politics will have on the political folk-ways. One probable effect is already evident, and it is not for the better."[25]

The *Times* followed with a second editorial criticizing the "Would Be Militants," stating that the exchange "certainly was not proper. The President of the United States is not to be heckled or hectored or made a defendant." While the editorial did not name Dorr, she was the implied target of the criticism.

It commended Shaw's brand of suffrage for its "good humor and moderation" that had won victories for their cause.

"This state of affairs, however, is obnoxious to those women who are temperamentally akin to the wild women of England," said the *Times*, comparing the Congressional Union to Pankhurst (with whom Dorr had worked).[26]

The confrontation failed to change Wilson's mind. In 1916, he told the convention of the National Woman Suffrage Association that he felt that the suffrage cause, 'so dear to his heart," had made wonderful progress since 1848 and could afford to wait longer.[27] In 1916 both major parties adopted "cautious suffrage planks" but the Democrats supported only the state-by-state method. Following the Democratic convention, the Congressional Union reorganized as the "aggressively political" National Woman's Party.[28]

Women began picketing the White House (a story recounted by Omaha native Doris Stevens in her book, *Jailed for Freedom*), and finally Wilson bowed to popular pressure. In 1917, he advised members of a House committee to vote for the amendment "as an act of right and justice to the women of the country and of the world."[29] Still the amendment remained stuck in Congress until 1919 when a Republican majority sent it to the states for ratification.[30] Dorr credited the Woman's Party for its approval in 1920.

"Those women started without a dollar in money, with every man's hand against them, with the only regularly organized suffrage group opposed to them, with a President openly hostile, and a Congress composed of men either opposed to them or believing sincerely that woman suffrage should come by State and not Federal action." She predicted that the women's movement would not "slow down" until American women gained "legal and social equality with men."[31]

Dorr herself continued to lead an unconventional life until her death in 1947. Among other adventures, she covered an all-female "battalion of death" during the Russian revolution. She tried to become a war correspondent covering the American army during World War I but was confronted by her "old sex handicap." With the help of Gen. John Pershing, commander of the American Expeditionary Force (whose sister edited a newspaper in Lincoln), she got just behind the front lines and was able to visit her son.[32]

After the war, she lived in Europe writing books, including her 1924 autobiography. She also dreamed of what the future would bring to women.

"The women of the future—the women whose feet we set on the path of progress—have a better chance to be good mothers, good wives and good citizens than we ever had."[33]

Eileen Wirth is a professor emeritus of journalism at Creighton University and a current member of History Nebraska's Board of Trustees. She is the author of From Society Page to Front Page: Nebraska Women in Journalism *(University of Nebraska Press).*

Doris Stevens

Nebraska's Forgotten Suffrage Leader

by Sally Bisson-Best

Doris Stevens: Nebraska's Forgotten Suffrage Leader
by Sally Bisson-Best

When the Nineteenth Amendment was ratified in August 1920, it marked the end of a decades-long struggle for women in the United States to be given the right to vote in all elections. From the Seneca Falls Convention in 1848 to the founding of the National Woman's Party in 1916, women such as Susan B. Anthony, Elizabeth Cady Stanton, and Alice Paul were well known leaders in the suffrage movement. Although they deserve much of the credit for the passage of the amendment, a prominent Nebraska native was also instrumental in its success. Her name was Doris Stevens, and in addition to her work for passage of the Nineteenth Amendment, she worked internationally for women's equality throughout her life. Although she was one of the most distinguished women of her time, she is not well known in her native state.

Doris Stevens was born in Omaha in 1888, and grew up in a house at 3961 Charles Street. Her parents, Caroline and Harry Stevens, moved to Nebraska from Ohio; they raised their four children in Omaha and remained there for the rest of their lives. Doris was their second daughter. Her parents were politically active and encouraged their children to be involved in civic affairs.[1] Stevens graduated from Omaha High School, now known as Central High School, in the class of 1905. She was a class officer, an editor of the school newspaper, and a talented musician.[2] She received a music scholarship to attend Oberlin College in Ohio, the first college to admit women. Stevens arrived on campus at age sixteen with a "brilliant scholarship, a rifle for shooting jack rabbits, a detestation for fudge parties and feminine gossip, and twenty two dollars borrowed from her brother."[3] She taught music lessons to help pay for her education, and was known as a spirited woman who occasionally flaunted the rules on campus by riding in a surrey with her dates after hours.[4]

During her college years, she became interested in women's suffrage. Stevens also met Sylvia Pankhurst, who came to Oberlin to speak. Pankhurst was British, and the daughter of the leader of the suffrage movement in England, Emmaline Pankhurst. While American women were lobbying, speaking, and working in individual states to gain the vote, the Pankhursts were employing more aggressive tactics, including throwing rocks at Parliament and burning buildings.[5] Their motto, "deeds, not words," was the rallying cry for their movement, and Alice Paul adopted some of their tactics.[6] Sylvia Pankhurst's advocacy brought her to the United States, where she spoke throughout the country and encouraged American women to work for a national suffrage amendment rather than a state-by-state approach.[7]

Stevens received her bachelor's degree in 1911, and worked as a teacher and social worker. She received favorable coverage in the local newspaper during this time. Under the headline "Omaha Girl Takes Degree," her graduation from Oberlin was highlighted in the *Omaha World-Herald*, which mentioned her excellent work in her Spanish, English, and sociology classes, as well as her piano and voice courses.[8] Her first jobs were working with children in the tenements of Cleveland, Ohio, and as the vice principal of a high school.[9] In 1913, she started working full time with Alice Paul as part of the Congressional Union, a subcommittee of the National American Woman Suffrage Association (NAWSA). Paul and Stevens were part of a new generation of suffrage leaders who believed the movement needed updated tactics, especially more publicity. One of their first events was a parade in Washington, D.C., in January 1913, on the same date as Woodrow Wilson's inauguration. Members of the Congressional Union also met with President Wilson, organized speakers, and lobbied Congress to raise awareness of the suffrage issue. Disagreements with NAWSA led Alice Paul to form the National Woman's Party (NWP) in 1916 with the sole platform of passing a federal suffrage amendment.[10] Doris Stevens worked closely with Paul in the formation of the NWP and was a member of the executive committee of that organization and the Congressional Union.[11]

Stevens spoke throughout the country on behalf of suffrage, and worked full time in the NWP's Washington, D.C., office. The *Omaha World-Herald* continued to cover her activities, but they began writing about her

Left: Doris Stevens, ca. 1919. Library of Congress

in less flattering terms, including referring to her as a "militant suffragist."[12] The change in tone reflected the strong local sentiment against the suffrage movement, which began in the late 1800s, before Stevens was born. A group of Nebraska women, notably Clara Bewick Colby, helped place a state constitutional amendment on the ballot in 1882. They also hosted Susan B. Anthony as a speaker. Anthony was aware that the local liquor lobby would be vocally opposed to suffrage, fearing that women voters would support temperance.[13] The amendment was defeated by a wide margin. Later attempts to pass a state suffrage law were vigorously opposed by the state's ethnic minorities, who valued personal liberty. Nebraska Germans were the state's largest ethnic minority in the early twentieth century, and their political reach was vast due to the large number of German language newspapers and community associations.[14] There were also a large number of breweries whose owners feared women voters would support prohibition, and some, notably Senator John Mattes from Nebraska City, led a coalition in the state senate that opposed both suffrage and prohibition.[15] When the United States declared war on Germany in April 1917, a wave of anti-German sentiment swept the country. In order to preserve a law that allowed German to be taught in the public schools, Mattes compromised and supported a limited suffrage amendment that was passed by the Nebraska legislature.[16] A referendum petition was filed by suffrage opponents with ties to the liquor industry, who obtained forged signatures to get the measure on the ballot. The validity of the referendum petition signatures was the subject of a lawsuit, which suffrage supporters won.[17] These issues were rendered moot by the passage of the federal suffrage amendment.

In addition to her advocacy work, one of Stevens's most significant contributions developed from a series of events in 1917. Frustrated with a lack of progress, NWP members began picketing the White House, holding banners asking President Wilson to support the Nineteenth Amendment.[18] Called the Silent Sentinels, the women picketed on a sidewalk in front the White House six days a week, regardless of the weather or the taunts of observers. Controversially, the picketing continued even after the United States entered World War I.[19]

In 1917, D.C. police began arresting the picketers on the questionable grounds of obstructing traffic.[20] The women were sent to the Occaquaon Workhouse, where they were mistreated. Stevens was arrested, and although she was released in a few days, she recorded these events in great detail in her book, *Jailed for Freedom*. Published in 1920, the book chronicles the events leading up to the picketing, the treatment the women received in the workhouse, and lists the names and hometowns of every woman who was arrested. Her chapter entitled *Prison Episodes* describes some of their maltreatment:

> They learned of that barbarous punishment known as the "greasy pole" used upon the girl prisoners. This method of punishment consisted of strapping girls with their hands tied behind them to a greasy pole from which they were partly suspended. Unable to keep themselves in an upright position, because of the grease on the pole, they slipped almost to the floor, with their arms all but severed from their arm sockets, suffering intense pain for long periods of time. This cruel punishment was meted out to prisoners for slight infractions of prison rules.[21]

The women also asked to be treated as political prisoners, which would have reduced the length of their sentences and severity of their treatment. This request was denied, and in response several of the women went on hunger strikes, a tactic that was successfully used by Sylvia Pankhurst in England.[22] Prison officials feared the hunger strikers would die, and resorted to force feeding them raw eggs through tubes inserted into their throats. Stevens recounted the force feeding and believed it was the first time a long, organized hunger strike was used for political purposes in the United States.[23]

Stevens's personal life was also affected by her work in the suffrage movement. She met her first husband, Dudley Field Malone, while she was traveling on behalf of the NWP. Malone was an attorney, had served as an Assistant United States Secretary of State, and was a personal friend of President Woodrow Wilson. Their initial meeting was in 1916 while they were both speaking at a suffrage event in California.[24] In 1917, Malone helped represent some of the women who were arrested for picketing the White

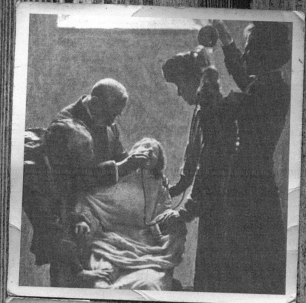

Top Left: Force-feeding an English suffragette. From Sylvia Pankhurst, *The Suffragette: The History of the Women's Militant Suffrage Movement, 1905-1910* (New York: Sturgis & Walton, 1911), p. 433. Pankhurst and the suffragette movement in Britain inspired Americans such as Alice Paul and Doris Stevens to take a more confrontational approach—and suffer similar brutality at the hands of authorities.

Top Right: Left to right: Doris Stevens, Alison Turnbull Hopkins, and Eunice Dana Brannan in prison dress. The women were arrested for picketing the White House on July 14, 1917, and sentenced to sixty days in Occoquan Workhouse; President Wilson pardoned them after three days. *Library of Congress*

Bottom Left: Doris Stevens, right, at the US Capitol for an event honoring Susan B. Anthony's birthday, February 15, 1939. Stevens was then involved in well-publicized dispute with President Franklin Roosevelt, who had just ousted her (illegally, Stevens said) from her longtime position as chair of the Inter-American Commission for Women. Stevens supported an equal rights amendment; her replacement favored "protective laws" for women instead. *Library of Congress*

Bottom Right: Right: Doris Stevens (standing, second from right), with Alice Paul (standing, right) and other suffrage leaders. *Library of Congress*

House, including Stevens. They were a well-known and prominent couple, and when they wed in 1921, the story was featured in both the *Omaha World-Herald* and the *New York Times*.[25] They moved to Paris, where Stevens began working for international women's equality and Malone practiced law. In keeping with her views on marriage and equality, Stevens kept her maiden name. This was also a newsworthy event, and the letter she wrote to her mother requesting that she continue to refer to her as Doris Stevens, without using Miss or Mrs. in her salutation, was featured in the press.[26]

Malone was notable beyond his representation of suffrage workers. Although he was primarily a divorce attorney, he also helped represent the defendant in the infamous case of *State of Tennessee v. John T. Scopes,* more commonly known as the Scopes Monkey Trial. As co-counsel with Clarence Darrow, Malone was noted for his oratorical skills and persuasive rhetoric, with prosecutor William Jennings Bryan praising one of Malone's speeches as one of the finest he had ever witnessed.[27] This is particularly noteworthy since Darrow and Bryan were considered extremely gifted orators in the courtroom.

Although Stevens and Malone were committed to the same issues, the marriage ended in divorce. Stevens filed the petition in Paris in 1927, and was granted the divorce two years later on the grounds of abandonment.[28] In her initial court filing, she asserted that their strong personalities made it impossible to sustain the marriage. Stevens did not ask for alimony because she believed it should only be awarded if minor children were involved in the divorce.[29]

For most of her adult life, Stevens lived in New York, but she visited her parents often. While her divorce from Malone was pending, she visited Omaha in 1927. In an interview with the *Omaha World-Herald* before the event, she extolled the virtues of the Midwest and mentioned she would like to study law at Columbia, the school closest to her New York home, but they did not admit women.[30] During this trip, she stayed at her parents' Omaha home, but also visited her sister, Alice Burns, in Elwood, Nebraska, and her brother, Ralph Stevens, in McCook.

In Omaha several days later she gave a controversial speech at a women's luncheon held in her honor. She said she didn't believe in separate women's and men's groups, such as the Women's Chamber of Commerce, whose president was one of the hosts of the event. "The only fun we get in life… is by men and women working and playing together. I am death on auxiliaries and stag parties."[31] She also asserted that women suffered from inferiority complexes due to the lack of equality in their lives. She believed that the origins of this inferiority came from historic oppression of women. "In primitive society, women were said to be possessed of the devil… and all evils were attributed to them, including famine, plagues, droughts and storms."[32] She told the audience that these longstanding beliefs prevented women from fully participating in all aspects of society, and advocated for change.

The fallout from her speech was swift, with attendees noting their shock and disagreement in subsequent interviews in the *Omaha World-Herald.* "I do not agree with Miss Stevens," said Miss Belle Ryan, assistant superintendent of education. "I think women are suffering more from a lack of popular evaluation of their real abilities. They have not had sufficient opportunity to make comparison with men in common fields of activity."[33] Margaret Doorly, a literary critic, believed Stevens made broad generalizations without providing context in terms of where and when a woman lived.[34] Mary E. La Roca, president of the Woodmen Circle, echoed Ryan's views. "There are wonderful opportunities for women," she said, "and it's possible those may feel inferior who have never availed themselves of them."[35] Stevens was also interviewed for this article, and offered additional reasons for her beliefs. She referred to scientific studies of the human brain, and clarified that she was not referring to all women. "Outstanding women in professional fields are always exceptions to the rule. I was speaking about the great mass of women in the home, who are made to feel inferior by the church, state, community and custom."[36]

The following week, Stevens spoke to the Chamber of Commerce Women's Division and attempted to further explain her remarks. She also expressed her affection for Omaha, noting it was where she received her early education.[37] She reiterated that she believed that society cast women in inferior roles, and that equal employment opportunities and equal pay were important for women to continue moving forward.[38] There isn't a record of the audience reaction to this speech. Stevens returned to New York, and continued working for women's equality, especially for passage of the Equal Rights Amendment, which was a focus of many former suffrage leaders after passage of the Nineteenth Amendment.

Stevens also had an interest in international women's equality. She was part of a US delegation that joined English suffrage supporters in a parade in London, where women were not allowed to vote until age thirty, while men could do so at twenty-one.[39] Her most significant accomplishment, however, was as the chair of the Inter-American Commission of Women from 1929 to 1937. Her work led to the passage of a treaty which extended women's equality to countries in Latin America. In recognition of her work, a banquet was held in New York in 1934, with over 200 prominent people in the audience.[40] Attendees included politicians, academics, and representatives from several countries involved in the agreement.[41] During her remarks, Stevens stated: "We shall see to it… that nothing less than equal treatment for women is henceforth permitted to enter international law from any source."[42]

Although her accomplishments were extensive, Stevens became less active in political issues later in her life. Political differences led to her removal from the Inter-American Commission, and she also left the NWP after an acrimonious dispute.[43] She did find a happy second marriage to journalist Jonathon Mitchell, whom she wed in 1935. They lived in New York, where Stevens began writing music about her childhood. With titles such as "When Father Made Rootbeer" and "Lake Manawa," her songs reflected her fond memories of growing up in Nebraska.[44] As she began organizing her personal records, she decided to donate some material to the Nebraska State Historical Society (today's History Nebraska), where she maintained a lifetime membership. In correspondence dated July 28, 1958, she wrote that she was beginning to organize her papers.[45] She also provided a copy of *Jailed for Freedom*, and audio recordings of three of her songs. All of her donated songs were based on growing up in Nebraska, and she offered the following comments:

> "Susie's May Basket" recalls a happy
> custom of my childhood in Omaha and how I

felt at a tender age toward the boy next door on Charles Street; "Nellie, My Darling" is a remembered experience from unforgettable days when Mother and Father took us on the trolley to the band concerts in Hanscom Park, Omaha; "Red Peony" is a tribute to my dear father, Henry H. Stevens, and attempts to reveal how I felt on the occasion of his sudden death and during the funeral ceremony in Omaha in 1930.[46]

Most of her personal papers, however, were donated to the Schlesinger Library that is part of the Radcliffe Institute for Advanced Study at Harvard University.[47] This library is devoted to women's history, which Stevens supported as an academic pursuit. Her second husband was a Harvard alumnus, which may have influenced her decision. In recognition of her lifelong work for women's equality, in 1986 her estate donated $1 million to establish an endowed chair in women's studies at Princeton University. The Doris Stevens Professorship is awarded annually to a feminist scholar.[48]

Although Stevens faded from being mentioned by local media, newspaper coverage of her fiftieth high school reunion was complimentary. She was one of the six members of the Omaha High School Class of 1905, four men and two women, highlighted in an article about prominent members of her class who were listed in editions of *Who's Who*.[49] The article noted that she was popular and well known in high school, and that she had worked for women's suffrage and equality throughout the world.[50]

Although Stevens was a woman of accomplishment and stature, she is relatively unknown in Nebraska. This may be due to her suffrage work, and the strong local opposition to women obtaining the vote. Some of her views on women's equality were not in the mainstream of society, and she readily expressed them regardless of audience or event. *Jailed for Freedom* was out of print for many years, and her visits to Omaha declined following the death of her parents. Her coverage in local newspapers may also have affected the way she was viewed. From the local girl who obtained her college degree, to the militant suffragist and unconventional spouse who kept her maiden name, she was portrayed in a very different light than most of the women of her generation.

Doris Stevens died in New York at the age of seventy on March 22, 1963. Although she has been deceased for many years, her work for women's equality continues to have a positive impact on women today. Her death was reported in the *Omaha World-Herald* where she was a referred to as a noted feminist.[51]

This article appeared in the Summer 2019 issue of Nebraska History. *Sally Bisson-Best, J.D., is director of the Legal Studies Program and associate professor of legal studies at the College of Saint Mary in Omaha.*

12-Star Suffrage Flag, 1911-1917

This flag from the Nebraska History Museum collections bears a star for each of the states in which women had gained full voting rights. (States granting only limited voting rights—including Nebraska—did not earn a star.)

The stars are applied in a variety of techniques. Six are applied with large hand stitches, with the raw edge of the fabric exposed (the other stars have the edges turned under). On the flag's reverse side, the blue field is cut out behind these stars so that they are visible from both front and back. Of the remaining stars, three are applied with both machine and hand stitching, two with machine stitching only, and one with small hand stitching and whip-stitching around the edges. There is some variation in the stars' fabric as well.

Apparently different people added the stars year by year. The above groupings seem to match groups of states: California became the sixth state to grant women the vote in 1911, joining Wyoming, Colorado, Utah, Idaho, and Washington. Next came Arizona, Kansas, and Oregon (1912); Montana and Nevada (1914); and New York (1917).

No further stars were added when Michigan, Oklahoma, and South Dakota joined the club in 1918. Perhaps this was due to World War I; the keepers of this flag may have been busy with Red Cross work by then. And after the war, suffragists' focus was no longer on state voting rights, but on the state-by-state ratification of the 19th Amendment.
HN 4622-14

Barkley vs. Pool: Woman Suffrage and the Nebraska Referendum Law

by James E. Potter

Nebraska suffragists had reason to rejoice when Governor Keith Neville, on April 21, 1917, signed a legislative act allowing women to vote in municipal elections and for presidential electors. Though not the full suffrage measure Nebraska women had been seeking, the law was a major breakthrough after decades of frustration and defeat. The legislature granted woman suffrage to the fullest extent possible under the state constitution, which continued to bar females from voting for most state officers. As the suffrage movement gained strength in Nebraska and elsewhere, it seemed likely that remaining constitutional barriers to full voting privileges for women would soon be eliminated.

A chill invaded this climate of optimism when it was learned that anti-suffrage forces planned to mount a referendum petition drive to force suspension of the new, limited suffrage law. After it became obvious that enough signatures had been gathered to suspend the law, the suffragists decided to seek an injunction to prevent the referendum from being placed on the ballot. During the next two years the Nebraska suffrage battle was waged in the courtroom. The case of *Barkley vs. Pool* eventually reached the Nebraska Supreme Court, which upheld a lower court ruling that the referendum petition drive had failed due to fraudulent and illegal procedures used in gathering signatures.

The decision in *Barkley vs. Pool* came too late to provide many opportunities for Nebraska women to vote. The suffrage law had been suspended while the case was in the courts. By the time the case was decided, the adoption of full suffrage amendments to the Nebraska and US constitutions was imminent. However, by discrediting the anti-suffrage forces, *Barkley vs. Pool* helped pave the way for the Nebraska Legislature's unanimous ratification of the federal suffrage amendment in August 1919. More importantly, the case demonstrated what appeared to be serious flaws in the statutes governing the initiative and referendum process. Because of the evidence presented by the suffragists in *Barkley vs. Pool,* the legislature in 1919 made more restrictive the legal requirements for circulating initiative or referendum petitions.[1] It is interesting to note that some of the changes enacted by the 1919 legislature resurfaced as key issues in debate over the constitutionality of the petition law, sparked by a failed 1986 initiative petition drive.

It was ironic that the groups seeking to prevent woman suffrage employed the referendum, which was a progressive reform anti-suffragists traditionally had opposed. No organization was more hostile to woman suffrage than the German-American Alliance, whose opposition was related to ethnic and religious values. Not

HERE! TAKE THE CHEE-ILD. WITH GOOD CARE IT WILL GROW

Nebr. Court

LIMITED SUFFRAGE

Nebraska Women Suffragists

Powell

" BY ORDER OF THE COURT "
—*Omaha Bee*

only did many German-Americans believe that a woman's place was in the home, but they feared that women voters would favor prohibition, a heartfelt issue for an ethnic group that generally regarded the drinking of alcoholic beverages as a matter of personal choice. The German-American Alliance was suspicious of the 1912 initiative and referendum amendments to the Nebraska constitution precisely because it feared that these constitutional weapons might be used by advocates of woman suffrage or prohibition to place such issues on the ballot.[2]

The Alliance's fears were realized when an initiative petition drive succeeded in placing a woman suffrage amendment on the ballot for the 1914 general election. The anti-suffrage forces could not have felt much relief when the amendment lost by less than 10,000 votes.[3] Compared to earlier elections where suffrage had been defeated four to one, the 1914 vote demonstrated that the suffrage movement was gaining momentum. Much worse was to come, however, when a prohibition amendment, added to the ballot by initiative in 1916, was approved in the general election by a majority of nearly 30,000 votes. Prohibition took effect on May 1, 1917, after the legislature passed enabling legislation.[4]

Complicating the political situation for Nebraskans of German descent was the outbreak of war in Europe in 1914. As the ostensibly neutral United States moved closer to the Allied camp and war with Germany loomed, Nebraskans with ties to the fatherland sought to protect threatened cultural prerogatives, some of which had been confirmed by statute. One was the Mockett Law, which authorized foreign language instruction in the public schools.[5] As anti-German sentiment increased in Nebraska, a movement to repeal the Mockett Law surfaced during

WHO

and

WHAT

WERE

BACK

of the

OPPOSITION

in

NEBRASKA?

BACKBONE!

the 1917 legislative session. This session, coinciding with American entry into the war, found the German-American members of the legislature increasingly on the defensive. In order to prevent repeal of the Mockett Law, German-stock lawmakers allegedly struck a deal to support the limited suffrage bill in return for votes from suffrage supporters to save the Mockett Law.[6]

Others besides German-Americans had reason to fear woman suffrage and its implications for political reform. They included men like Omaha boss Tom Dennison, whose empire depended on bootlegging, gambling, and

Above:
On January 24, 1919, Judge Flansburg issued an injunction against the referendum to repeal the limited suffrage law. *Omaha Evening Bee*, January 27, 1919.

Opposite:
From *The Woman Citizen*, February 8, 1919.

prostitution. The Dennison machine was already facing stiff opposition from Omaha reformers without opening the voting booth to women. To people like Dennison, woman suffrage in municipal elections presented a clear threat to the political status quo.[7]

After the 1917 legislature adjourned, a coalition of anti-suffrage forces made plans to defeat the limited

Left and Center: By checking thousands of signatures, suffrage workers Katherine Sumney (left) and Grace Richardson (center) uncovered fraud in the 1917 anti-suffrage referendum petition drive. Years later, Richardson compiled the suffrage materials they collected into a set of scrapbooks donated to History Nebraska. HN RG1073.AM

Right: Nebraska Secretary of State Charles W. Pool. HN RG2411-4414-3

suffrage law through the referendum process. If sufficient signatures could be gathered, the law would be suspended until it could be submitted to a vote of the people at the 1918 general election. Though there was no certainty that voters would reject the law, at least women would be barred from voting in the various municipal elections scheduled during the ensuing year and a half.

The initiative and referendum, publicized and popularized by such reformers as William Jennings Bryan, had been added to the Nebraska constitution by a vote of the all-male electorate in 1912. The amendment established the basis for calculating the number of signatures of legal voters required on petitions but gave the legislature responsibility for specifying the mechanics of the initiative and referendum process.[8] The 1913 legislature affirmed that those signing initiative or

Under the provisions of the 1913 referendum law, the anti-suffrage forces were required to gather 29,147 signatures within ninety days after the 1917 legislature adjourned in order to suspend the limited suffrage law for submission to a vote of the people. A group known as the Nebraska Association Opposed to Woman Suffrage, headquartered in Omaha, took the lead in the petition drive. This group allegedly was supported by various Omaha politicians, by the German-American Alliance, and by liquor interests.[10] Probably for the sake of appearance, the organization's leadership included a number of women opposed to woman suffrage.[11]

Some newspapers questioned whether there was much support for the anti-suffrage position. The *Nebraska State Journal* doubted that 30,000 men would be willing to go on record in favor of depriving women of voting privileges already granted by the legislature. The newspaper castigated the anti-suffragist "diehards" for their efforts at a time when women were being "asked to fight for a country which will not grant them the responsibilities of citizenship."[12] This sentiment was echoed by others including the editor of the *North Nebraska Eagle* of Dakota City:

> It should be known by anyone solicited to sign this petition that it has the legal effect of suspending the law for two years and is equivalent to denying to the women of Nebraska the small part in the government that the legislature gave them. If you believe in suffrage refuse to sign such a petition. It requires 30,000 names and the Eagle does not believe there are that many men in Nebraska who will openly declare themselves so unfair.[13]

referendum petitions had to be legal voters. Presumably legal voters were those meeting the constitutional definition of "elector," that is, white males, at least twenty-one years of age, either citizens or aliens who had declared their intention to become citizens. The 1913 law was silent regarding qualifications for petition circulators. Apparently they did not have to be legal voters, literate, or even Nebraska residents. Circulators of petitions were required to certify that the petitioners had signed in the circulator's presence and that the circulator believed the information given by the petitioner was correct. It was a felony for anyone to sign a petition with other than his own name; to knowingly sign more than once for the same issue; or to sign when not a legal voter. Circulators could be charged with a felony for falsely certifying to the signatures on any petition.[9]

Despite observers' skepticism about the petition drive's chances for success, signatures were collected without apparent difficulty. On July 21, 1917, anti-suffrage leader Mrs. L. B. Crofoot, whose husband was president of the anti-prohibition "Prosperity League," presented petitions containing over 32,000 signatures to Secretary of State Charles W. Pool. The ease with which the signatures had been gathered aroused the suspicions of the Nebraska Woman Suffrage Association. Suffragists grew even more suspicious when newspapers reported that circulators had been paid for signatures gathered in Omaha pool halls and "soft drink" parlors, and that petition circulators had represented the petition as a pro-suffrage document.[14]

After determining that the required number of signatures had been collected, the secretary of state announced his intention to place the referendum on the ballot for the November 1918 general election. The law did not require that he verify the validity of the petitions, stipulating only that he determine whether they contained enough signatures. Citizens who wished to challenge the petitions could, under the initiative and referendum statutes, seek an injunction against the secretary of state in Lancaster County District Court.[15]

On July 28, 1917, Mrs. Edna Barkley, president of the Nebraska Woman Suffrage Association, asked Secretary of State Pool for permission to examine the anti-suffrage petitions. At first Pool refused, offering to provide copies; later he gave representatives of the association free access to the petitions.[16]

The suffragists planned to challenge the petitions on the basis of fraud. Because 18,000 of the more than 30,000 signatures were gathered in Omaha, it was there that they decided to concentrate their efforts. In September 1917 members of the association began working to verify names and addresses.[17] By mid-February 1918 the suffragists were ready to go to court in an effort to prove that the referendum petition drive had failed.

An anti-suffrage referendum petition (front and back), believed to include fraudulent signatures written by the same person. HN RG2

Top: "I am not ashamed to tell you that I am 63, although many take me for 20 years more than my real age," Mrs. Smith told the election commissioner. "Why not just put me down as short, stout, and gray?" It was a running joke among anti-suffragists that women would not register if they had to give their real age. *Omaha Bee*, May 28, 1919. HN RG 1073.AM.S5.F9

Bottom: Unlabeled clipping from one of Grace Richardson's scrapbooks. HN RG 1073.AM.S5.F9

Girls, If You Want to Vote, Tell Your Exact Weight, Height, and Worst of All---Age

Mesdames H. C. Sumney, James Richardson and Draper Smith First Women to Register.

Election Commissioner H. G. Moorhead is having the time of his life registering women for the first time in the history of Omaha to allow them to participate in the voting on the $3,000,000 Douglas county paving issue. The new blanks were received yesterday and the first registrants were: Mrs. H. C. Sumney and Mrs. James Richardson, president and second vice president, respectively, of the Political Equality League, and Mrs. Draper Smith, honorary president of the Nebraska Woman Suffrage association.

Mr. Moorhead was nervous when three women appeared before the counter and applied for registration. He endeavored to appear at ease, but he could not conceal his feelings.

No "Apparent" Age.

The blanks call for "apparent

Left to right: Election Commissioner Moorhead, Mrs. H. C. Sumney, Mrs. Draper Smith and Mrs. James Richardson.

Omaha Suffrage Leaders Become Real Citizens at Last and Celebrate Event by Taking Oath of Registration in Douglas County

Commissioner Moorhead Administers Oath to Mesdames Sumney, Smith and Richardson.

On February 18 Mrs. Barkley and eighteen co-plaintiffs filed suit in Lancaster County District Court. They asked Judge Leonard A. Flansburg for an injunction against Secretary of State Pool to prevent Pool from placing the referendum on the November general election ballot. The suffragists charged that the petitions violated the referendum law in several respects. The suit argued that many of the signatures on the petitions were not genuine, that many petitions were certified illegally, that some circulators had engaged in fraud to procure signatures, and that altogether the referendum petitions did not contain the number of genuine signatures required by law.[18]

On March 16 eighty-seven men and women active in the anti-suffrage ranks petitioned the court and were permitted to join the case as "intervenors." Judge Flansburg appointed a special examiner to take testimony regarding the authenticity of referendum petitions that had been circulated across the state.[19] The suffragists, who had spent long hours investigating petition signatures in Omaha and elsewhere, were ready to present their evidence.

As the hearings proceeded, it became clear that a final ruling in the case might not be made before the November 1918 election. The anti-suffragists hoped the delay might force the issue to a vote of the people regardless of the ongoing investigation. To prevent the secretary of state from placing the referendum on the November ballot the plaintiffs requested a temporary restraining order against Pool. Judge Flansburg issued the order on July 6, 1918.[20]

Throughout the summer and fall of 1918 the hearings dragged on. After being presented with convincing evidence that fraudulent signatures had been found on some of the petitions circulated in Omaha, Judge Flansburg decided to replace the restraining order with a temporary injunction against the secretary of state.[21]

The suffragists used a process as simple as it was time consuming to check the validity of signatures. They copied petitions filed with the secretary of state and tried to verify each name and address. Some 18,000 names were checked in Omaha by suffrage workers under the leadership of Mrs. Katherine Sumney and Mrs. Grace Richardson.[22] The workers found that many of the addresses on petitions were fictitious and that the localities named were in the middle of cornfields or railroad yards. Some addresses, had they existed, would have been located in the Missouri River. The suffragists discovered petitions bearing the names of men who had never lived at the addresses given and who, when contacted, affirmed that they had never signed any petition. Some men said that they had signed a petition because the circulator had represented it as a pro-suffrage petition; others thought it was a petition to "bring back beer." Paid circulators from Omaha traveled around the state collecting signatures. In at least one instance a circulator was a resident of Iowa. A person named A. O. Barclay had certified to 112 Douglas County petitions on which many of the signatures could not be verified. Despite the efforts of investigators, Barclay was never located.[23]

Handwriting experts testified that all signatures on many petitions were in the same handwriting. Other petitions were found to have been left in pool halls, cigar stores, and barber shops for anyone to sign. Some were circulated by minors or by illiterates who were paid a fee for each signature. In several instances, the plaintiffs proved that men whose signatures appeared on petitions had died months before the petitions were circulated. One Nebraska newspaper noted that "many dead and gone long before the suffrage question ever became an issue in Nebraska apparently returned to Earth to fight suffrage."[24] One Omaha petition contained the name of W. J. Bryan, residing at 1462 North Seventh Street. A search revealed no such address. The *Omaha Daily News* remarked, "If W. J. Bryan lived at that address he would be domiciled in the middle of Charles Street. Neighbors say to their knowledge Mr. Bryan has not lived in the street."[25]

One fact that was particularly galling to the suffragists was that many petition signers were not citizens. The Nebraska constitution provided that males who had declared their intention to become citizens (e.g. had taken out their "first papers") were "electors" and qualified to sign initiative or referendum petitions. It seemed poetic justice later when, just as the ruling in *Barkley vs. Pool* restored limited voting rights to women, a 1918 constitutional amendment prohibiting alien suffrage took effect, disenfranchising thousands who had never bothered to become citizens.[26]

In issuing the temporary injunction, Judge Flansburg ruled that the plaintiffs had proved that many of the names on specific petitions had been fraudulently written there by the circulators. Therefore those entire petitions would be disqualified unless the intervenors could prove that the remaining signatures were genuine. However, except for generally denying knowledge of any fraud, the anti-suffrage leaders made no effort to refute the testimony of the plaintiffs. They convinced Judge Flansburg to issue a special finding that the Omaha women who directed the circulation of the petitions had not been shown to have been implicated in the frauds![27] After the temporary injunction was issued, the anti-suffrage forces appealed to the Nebraska Supreme Court, which refused to hear the appeal on the grounds that the district court injunction was not a final order in the case.[28]

On January 24, 1919, Judge Flansburg issued a permanent injunction to prevent the secretary of state from submitting the limited suffrage law to a vote of the people. The judge found that fraud, forgery, and false certification invalidated more than 4,600 signatures on the referendum petitions and that the required number of valid signatures had not been collected. He assessed the costs in the case to the state (as defendant) and to the intervenors. The Nebraska attorney general ruled that women were eligible to vote in upcoming municipal elections under the provisions of the 1917 limited suffrage law.[29]

On April 28 the intervenors appealed Judge Flansburg's ruling to the Nebraska Supreme Court while the state, having accepted the decision, withdrew from the case. The intervenors appealed on the grounds that the judge had erred in throwing out entire petitions when only certain names had been proved fraudulent, that the plaintiffs (who were not eligible to vote) had no right to sue because the suit pertained to a political, rather than a civil right; and that the injunction prevented the legal voters of the state from voting on the question of woman suffrage.[30]

In upholding Judge Flansburg's ruling the Supreme Court on June 28, 1919, agreed that the remedy of injunction against fraudulent referendum petitions was available to any citizen including non-voting women, and that knowingly certifying to a fraudulent signature on a referendum petition destroyed the credibility of the circulator to the degree that the entire petition was invalidated.[31]

In the aftermath of this protracted struggle the suffrage movement soon achieved final victory. On August 2, 1919, the Nebraska legislature in special session unanimously ratified the nineteenth amendment to the US Constitution. After ratification by other states the federal amendment took effect in August 1920. A Nebraska constitutional convention proposed a full suffrage amendment to the state constitution, which was approved by the votes of both men and women at a September 21, 1920, special election.[32]

Though the case of *Barkley vs. Pool* failed to materially hasten the enfranchisement of Nebraska women, it had a significant effect on the subsequent history of the state's initiative and referendum law. Even the suffragists recognized that the fate of woman suffrage did not hinge on the outcome of the case. Mrs. Grace Richardson noted:

> This has been a fight for good government even more than for the right of women in Nebraska to vote ... We were not afraid to have the suffrage question voted on again as has been suggested by some opponents of suffrage but we were unwilling to have it brought before the people by fraudulent petitions. The fight has been to protect state laws on the initiative and referendum.[33]

This view was echoed by the *Nebraska State Journal:*

> What happened can be told in a few words. A large fund of money was raised by interests opposed to suffrage. Men were given money and told to get the petitions. There was only

a pot of money. Men hired to get signatures found it hard to get signers. Some, accordingly, secured signatures by representing it as a pro-suffrage petition. Others took a short cut and signed up the petitions themselves, using city directories or telephone directories as a source of names. No other referendum petitions had been questioned as to their genuineness. It was assumed that this one would not be.

Could this kind of thing have continued, we should shortly have been at a point where anybody with ten thousand dollars to spend could buy the suspension of any act of the legislature... Manipulating referendum petitions is not a killing matter. The most that can be accomplished, if the people favor the legislation attacked, is a delay of a year and a half. Nevertheless, fraud, even of no worse consequence than this, is intolerable. The present legislature will no doubt consider whether ways cannot be found to render fraud in initiative and referendum petitions harder to commit and more certain of detection and punishment.[34]

As the *State Journal* predicted, the 1919 session of the Nebraska Legislature amended the law pertaining to the initiative and referendum. Senate File 225, adopted by a vote of 29-0 in the senate and 75-0 in the house, was approved by Governor Samuel McKelvie on April 16, 1919. The press reported that the new amendments to the initiative and referendum law were for the specific purpose of preventing fraud in the circulation of petitions. *The Woman Citizen,* the organ of the National Woman Suffrage Association, predicted that the amendments

will make impossible, as far as can be done, any such frauds in the future and warn corrupt individuals from trying thus to pervert the law ... (the amendments] will compel those who may file such petitions in the future to buttress them thoroughly against attack, or in other

words, stop the filing of referendum petitions that are fraudulent and perjured in character.[35]

Significant changes were made in the statutory provisions governing petition circulators. Where the old law was silent regarding circulators' qualifications, the amended law required that they be at least eighteen years of age and a resident of the county in which petitions were to be circulated. Furthermore, circulators were required to swear to the validity of the petitions rather than merely to certify. Each circulator was required to swear that he had stated the nature of the petition to each person asked to sign. Anyone wishing to circulate petitions outside their county of residence was required to give bond.[36]

Since 1919 Nebraska's initiative and referendum law has been amended several times. Later amendments have made even more restrictive the initiative and referendum process. Legislation in 1969 and 1973 prohibited paid circulators and required that petition signers be registered voters.[37] A failed 1986 initiative seeking a popular vote on a state lottery resulted in charges against several individuals on the grounds that they violated the petition law, certain provisions of which had been enacted by the 1919 legislature in response to the case of *Barkley vs. Pool.* The episode produced court challenges to the constitutionality of portions of the law and sparked debate over whether changes were needed.[38]

Though they could not yet vote, Nebraska suffragists made a significant contribution to Nebraska's political history through their fight against the referendum on the 1917 limited suffrage law. They demonstrated the fallacy of the anti-suffrage argument that women were "too delicate" for the rough and tumble world of politics. In order to protect a fundamental concept of direct democracy, they waged a lengthy and expensive legal battle more important in principle than for its eventual effect on the suffrage cause. By the time they won full suffrage, Nebraska women had already demonstrated that they were ready for, and capable of, full participation in the political process.

This article appeared in the Spring 1988 issue of Nebraska History. James E. Potter (1945-2016) worked for the Nebraska State Historical Society for nearly fifty years, serving in turn as archivist, editor, and senior research historian.

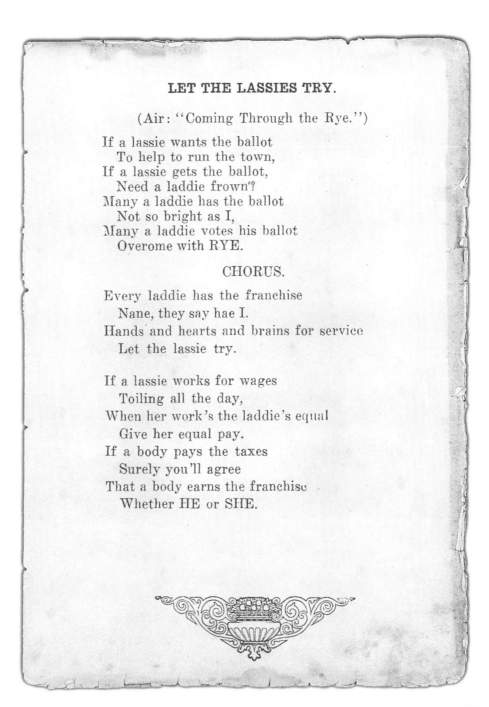

LET THE LASSIES TRY.

(Air: "Coming Through the Rye.")

If a lassie wants the ballot
　To help to run the town,
If a lassie gets the ballot,
　Need a laddie frown?
Many a laddie has the ballot
　Not so bright as I,
Many a laddie votes his ballot
　Overome with RYE.

CHORUS.

Every laddie has the franchise
　Nane, they say hae I.
Hands and hearts and brains for service
　Let the lassie try.

If a lassie works for wages
　Toiling all the day,
When her work's the laddie's equal
　Give her equal pay.
If a body pays the taxes
　Surely you'll agree
That a body earns the franchise
　Whether HE or SHE.

From Suffrage Songs brochure.
9255-23-(1)

Minnie Fisher Cunningham, suffragist and director of the League of Women Voters. RG3357. PH0-1719

Eli S. Ricker of Chadron, Nebraska, April 1916. The 73-year-old judge is wearing a "Votes for Women" button. An identical one shown as an inset is from the National Museum of American History collection, Smithsonian Institution. RG1227.PH1-2

DELEGATE

CONVENTION
NEBRASKA
WOMAN'S
CHRISTIAN
TEMPERANCE
UNION

LINCOLN
OCT. 15-18, '07

Many suffragists were also prohibitionists, which led liquor interests to oppose both prohibition and suffrage.

Far left: two badges are from the 1908 National Prohibition Convention.
HN Collection: 4480, 4481, 8045-63

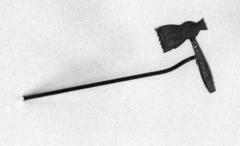

Prohibition activist and suffragist Carry A. Nation gained notoriety by vandalizing saloons with a hatchet. She sold hatchet pins (top) to help finance her crusades. She gave this one on to E.S. Augr, a railroad station agent in Exeter, when she stopped to send a telegram. HN Collection: 10376-1

Lincoln residents voted the city "dry" in 1909 by a narrow vote, and city voters reaffirmed the measure in 1910, even as the statewide prohibition movement heated up. HN Collection: 8661-126, 8661-308, 9805-524, 10506-85

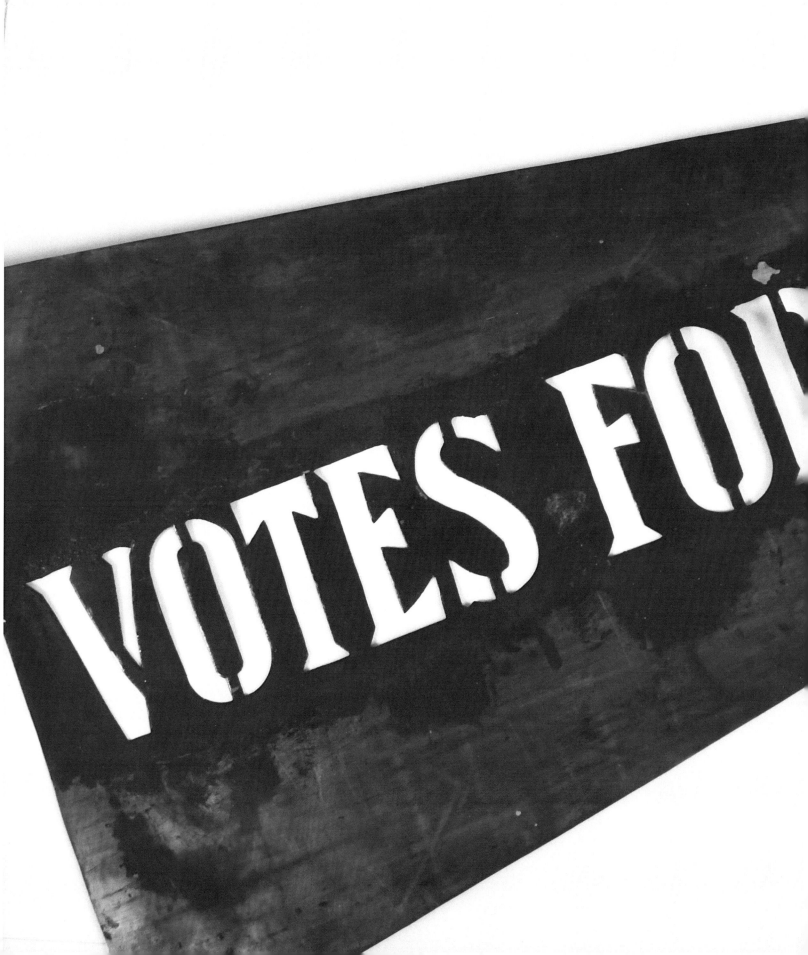

Above, brass stencil, undated.
HN Collection: 7428-1

Various suffrage buttons.
HN Collection: 4123-12, 7206-1-(8),
8661-128, 10443-489, 7206-1-(7)

VOTES FOR WOMEN
VOTES FOR WOMEN
VOTES FOR WOMEN
VOTES FOR WOMEN

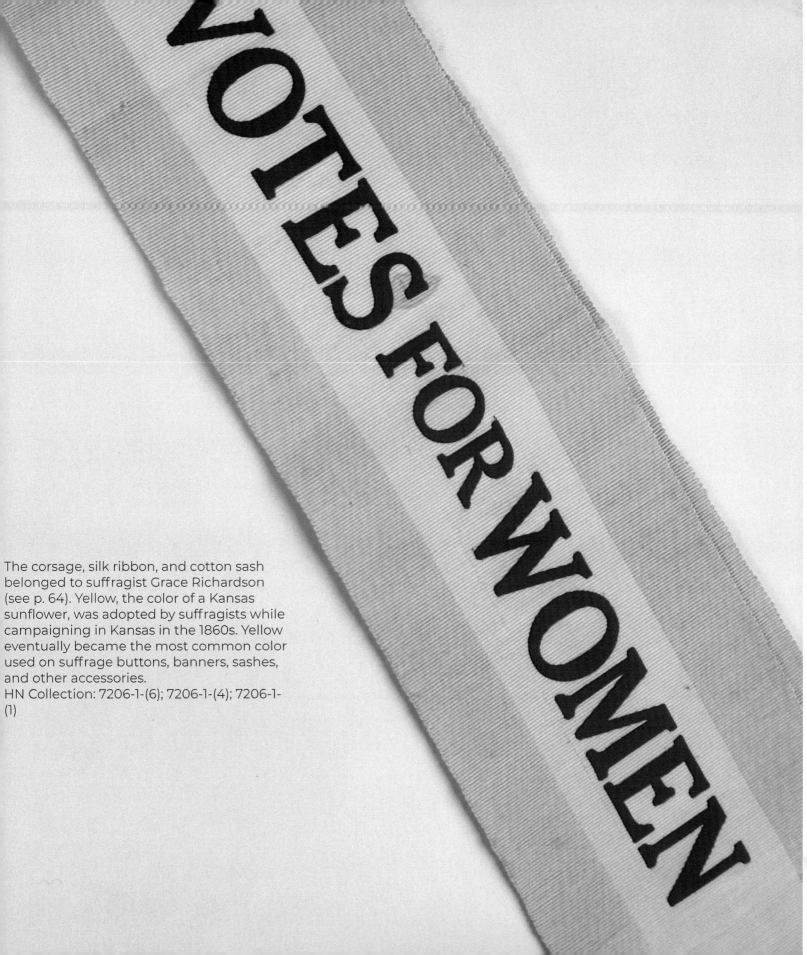

The corsage, silk ribbon, and cotton sash belonged to suffragist Grace Richardson (see p. 64). Yellow, the color of a Kansas sunflower, was adopted by suffragists while campaigning in Kansas in the 1860s. Yellow eventually became the most common color used on suffrage buttons, banners, sashes, and other accessories.
HN Collection: 7206-1-(6); 7206-1-(4); 7206-1-(1)

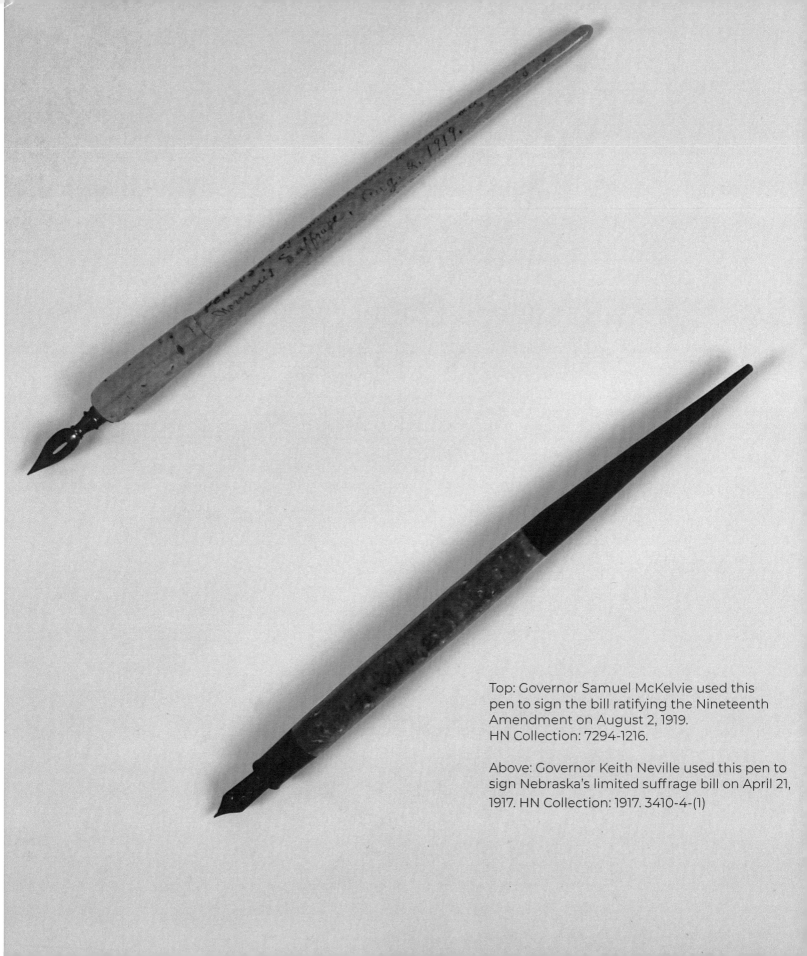

Top: Governor Samuel McKelvie used this pen to sign the bill ratifying the Nineteenth Amendment on August 2, 1919.
HN Collection: 7294-1216.

Above: Governor Keith Neville used this pen to sign Nebraska's limited suffrage bill on April 21, 1917. HN Collection: 1917. 3410-4-(1)

Artist/sculptor/feminist
Suzanne Benton created
this necklace and Susan B.
Anthony pendant in the 1970s.
HN Collection: 10057-3-(1-2)

Virginia Smith (1911-2006), represented Nebraska's Third District in the US House of Representatives from 1975 to 2001, the first Nebraska woman to hold a seat in the House. Helen Boosalis (1919-2009) was the first woman to serve as mayor of Lincoln, an office she held from 1975 to 1983.
HN Collection: 10965-10, 10965-8, 9601-73, 7294-6664

In the 1987 governor's race, Boosalis, a Democrat, faced off against Republican state treasurer Kay Orr. It was the first time in US history that women represented both major parties in a gubernatorial election. Orr won and became Nebraska's first female governor.
HN Collection: 13120,20, 13143-38, 10962-2, 13120-4

ORR MADDUX

KAY ORR

RE-ELECT SMITH TO CONGRESS

4 m'ORR

Nebraska was one of the last states west of the Mississippi to grant women the right to vote. Nebraska's suffragists often carried banners and pennants with the names of suffrage states as part of their "Nebraska Next" campaign.
HN Collection: 4622-8

Primary Sources: Women's Suffrage Resources at History Nebraska

Our website is a good starting point for research related to any aspect of Nebraska history, but many important resources are only available at our facility at 1500 R Street in Lincoln. In addition to general resources such as our extensive Nebraska newspaper collections and county and local histories, the following sources are of particular interest to researchers interested in the suffrage movement.

Manuscript Collections

Suffrage-related items are found in multiple collections. Here are the major ones. Finding aids are available at history.nebraska.gov (enter the "RG" number or collection name in the search window).

- RG1058.AM. Inez Celia Philbrick (1866-1966). The bulk of the collection consists of correspondence and printed matter relating to Dr. Philbrick's activities in support of women's suffrage, euthanasia, and education. (0.5 cu. ft.)

- RG1073.AM. Nebraska Woman Suffrage Association. The records (1888-1920, particularly 1910-20) include official business, media coverage, relationship to the national organization, and details of the 1917-19 court case, *Barkley vs. Pool*. (2.5 cu. ft.)

- RG1987.AM. League of Women Voters of Nebraska. Records, printed matter, 1919-1980s. Founded to help women exercise their new right to vote, the League's activities included researching, writing, and distributing information on the legislative and voting processes as well as the pros and cons of election issues. (20 cu. ft.)

- RG3740.AM. Doris Stevens (1892-1963). Manuscripts, printed matter, and sheet music by the Omaha-born suffragist. (0.25 cu. ft.)

- RG4054.AM. Harriet Sophia (Brewer) Brooks, 1828-1888. Brooks was a suffragist, newspaper columnist, and one of the founding members of the Nebraska Woman Suffrage Association. Her papers (mostly 1852-1888) include correspondence, articles and newspaper clippings, suffrage association records, and biographical information. (0.25 cu. ft.)

- RG4430.AM. Erasmus Michael Correll. Correll and his wife, Lucy, were ardent supporters of woman suffrage. Correll published the *Hebron Journal* and the *Western Woman's Journal*, the latter a nationally-known suffrage paper. Correll also served a term in Congress and was president of the American Woman's Suffrage Association. (0.5 cu. ft.)

Microfilm

History Nebraska has microfilm these relevant newspapers:

- *The Suffrage Messenger* (founded 1915). Monthly publication of the Nebraska Woman's Suffrage Association. 324.2 N27s

- *The Union Worker* (founded 1889). Published in Hastings by A. G. Fitch. Monthly suffrage publication. Film 324.3 H24uw

- *Western Woman's Journal* (founded 1881). Edited by Erasmus Correll, the Journal was "Devoted to and her home, industrial, educational, and legal interests—especially advocating woman suffrage." Film 396 W52

- *The Woman's Tribune* (1883-1909), the nation's second-longest-running suffrage newspaper, published in Beatrice, Nebraska (and later in Washington, DC, and Portland, OR) by Clara Bewick Colby. It began as the official paper of the Nebraska Woman Suffrage Association, and 1886-89 was the official paper of the National Woman Suffrage Association. It remains an important archival resource of the movement, preserving content not available elsewhere. Call number: Film 324.3 W84

Photographs and Artifacts

Too numerous to list; several are included in this publication. Many are cataloged at history.nebraska.gov/explore-collections. Search for "suffrage."

Notes

Wilhite, "Sixty-Five Years Till Victory: A History of Woman Suffrage in Nebraska"

1   Dexter Bloomer, *Life and Writings of Amelia Bloomer* (Boston: Arena Publishing Company, 1895), p. 159.

2   Quoted in Amelia Bloomer, "First Female Suffragist Movement in Nebraska," *Transactions and Reports of the Nebraska State Historical Society* (Lincoln, 1885), I, 59.

3   Dexter Bloomer, Life and Writings . . .p. 214.

4   Wyoming Territory granted full suffrage to women in 1869. Abroad, the first area to do so was the Isle of Man in 1881.

5   Amelia Bloomer, "First Female Suffragist .. ," p. 60. Andreas (*History of the State of Nebraska*, pp. 183-184) records the matter differently: "some of the members of the opposition proposed to present General Larimer with a petticoat as a badge of his devotion to the sex. After the lapse of a quarter of a century, it is safe to remark that such an emblem, had it really been imposed on the General at that time would now be regarded as an historic garment, worthy of preservation among the valued relics of the State." Did he or did he not receive a petticoat?

6   The March 1, 1881, school suffrage law has been effective to date. Electors must reside in the district and own taxable property therein or have children of school age.

7   Official Report of the Debates and Proceedings in the Nebraska Constitutional Convention, *Publications of the Nebraska State Historical Society* (York: 1871), XI, 121.

8   Ibid., XIII, 78. See particularly the arguments pp. 64-82, 124-146, 199-231 and 266-302.

9   Ibid., p. 130.

10   Ibid., p. 277.

11   Lucy Correll, "Suffrage in Nebraska," Nebraska Society of the Daughters of the American Revolution, *Collection of Nebraska Pioneer Reminiscences*, (Cedar Rapids, Iowa: The Torch Press, 1916), p. 277.

12   *Western Woman's Journal*, I (May, 1881),27, quoting the comments of *The Beatrice Express* on the new journal.

13   Ibid., p. 24.

14   *Western Woman's Journal,* 11 (September, 1882), 280, quoting *The Omaha Republican*.

15   *Nebraska Party Platforms, 1858-1940,* (Lincoln: University of Nebraska Press, 1940), p. 99.

16   *Western Woman's Journal*, I (April, 1881), 2.

17   *Omaha Herald*, October 1, 1882, p. 2.

18   J. Sterling Morton and Albert Watkins, *Illustrated History of Nebraska* (Lincoln: Jacob North and Company, 1907), III, 285.

19   Othman Abbott, "Struggle for Woman's Rights in Nebraska," *Nebraska History*, XI (July-September, 1928), 151.

20   Nebraska Party Platforms . . , p. 102.

21   Addison E. Sheldon, *Nebraska, the Land and the People* (Chicago: Lewis Publishing Company, 1931), I, 642-643.

22   Personal letter of Grace Mason Wheeler to Mrs. Mary Dennet, December 15, 1910. Nebraska State Historical Society, MS1073, Box 2.

23   Interview with Mrs. Ada Shafer (a Nebraska suffragette) in *The Omaha World-Herald*, September 15, 1966.

24   Proceedings of the Thirty-Third Session of the Nebraska House of Representatives (House Journal), (Lincoln: Jacob North and Company, 1913), pp.739-741.

25   "Outlook Is Bright," [n.d.] Newspaper clipping, presumably *The Lincoln Star*, in Nebraska State Historical Society, MS1058.

26   "Should Have Carried," *Suffrage Messenger*, II (July 1, 1916), 1.

27   See "Anti-Suffragists Plan Big Meeting Next Saturday," *Omaha Bee*, September 23, 1914, in MS1073, Box 1.

28   James Clifton Child, *The German-Americans in Politics*, 1914-1917, (University of Wisconsin, 1939), p. 17.

29   Letter to Local Alliance of Columbus from German-American Alliance, MS1073, Scrapbook 1, p. 21.

30   Personal letter of Mrs. Katherine Sumney to Mr. Charles Halliman, September 28, 1915, MS1073, Box 1.

31   *Omaha World-Herald*, September 15, 1966.

32   "Pig for Suffrage," *Suffrage Messenger*, I (November 1, 1915), 2.

33   "Plan for 1918 Suffrage Fight," *Omaha News*, May 5, 1916, MS1073, Box 1.

34   MS1073, Scrapbook 3 deals with the 1917 case.

35   "Nebraska Suffragists Win," *Woman Citizen*, IV (July 19, 1919), 168.

36   "Killed by Request of Suffrage Women," *Lincoln*

Journal, March 28, 1919. MS1073, Box 2.

37   An amendment granting suffrage to women was first submitted to Congress in 1875 by Miss Anthony. It was not introduced in the Senate until 1878 and was voted on four times before it passed. (See Congressional Record, LVIII, Pt. 1 [May 21, 1919], 83). In the fourth vote (February, 1919), the German-American Alliance was almost successful again in defeating suffrage. Nebraska's Senator Gilbert M. Hitchcock, supported by the Alliance, defied his constituents and voted against the amendment. Only one more positive vote would have made the necessary two-thirds majority.

38   *Messages and Proclamations of the Governors of Nebraska.* (Lincoln: Nebraska State Historical Society, 1942), III, 425.

Bristow, "Susan B. Anthony and the Abbott Sisters"

1   *Nebraska State Historical Society Manuscript Finding Aid, RG2916.AM: Abbott Family*, History Nebraska, history.nebraska.gov/ collections/abbott-family-rg2916am.

2   Othman A. Abbott, *Recollections of a Pioneer Lawyer* (Lincoln: Nebraska State Historical Society, 1929), 150. Quoted in "The Abbotts Play Host to Susan B. Anthony," *Nebraska Timeline* (February 2003), weekly column published by History Nebraska.

3   Presumably Vinemont, Alabama.

4   Elizabeth Cady Stanton, president of the National Woman Suffrage Association.

5   Members of Congress, apparently.

6   Letter from Susan B. Anthony to Elizabeth Abbott, Aug. 22, 1881. History Nebraska RG2916.AM, Series 4, Box 2, Folder 6.

7   Abbott, *Recollections of a Pioneer Lawyer*, 150.

Bloomberg , "'Striving for Equal Rights for All': Woman Suffrage in Nebraska 1855-188246"

1   Editor's note: To avoid repetition of material already covered in Ann Wiegman Wilhite's essay, this reprint omits a section summarizing the early history of the Nebraska women's suffrage movement.

2   Lucy L. Correll, "Suffrage in Nebraska," Collection of Nebraska Pioneer Reminiscences, Nebraska Society of the Daughters of the American Revolution (Cedar Rapids, Iowa: Torch Press, 1916), 277.

3   For biographical information on Harriet Sophia Brewer Brooks, see the biographical note for her papers RG4054.AM, NSHS.

4   "Mrs. Ada M. Bittenbender," *A Woman of the Century: Fourteen Hundred-Seventy Biographical Sketches Accompanied by Portraits of Leading American Women in All Walks of Life*, Frances E. Willard and Mary A. Livermore., eds., Vol. I (1893) (Facsimile Edition New York: Gordon Press, 1975), 87-88.

5   For biographical information on Erasmus Michael Correll, see the Manuscript Record overview of the Erasmus M. Correll Papers MS572, NSHS; also his biographical sketch in A.T. Andreas's *History of the State of Nebraska* (Chicago: Western Historical Co., 1882).

6   *Beatrice Express*, Dec. 11, p. 1, Dec. 21, p.1, 1876.

7   Ibid., Dec. 5 1872, p. 3, Apr. 16, 1874, p. 3. See also records of the Ladies' Library Association, Beatrice Public Library, Beatrice, Nebraska. *The Woman's Journal* ran from 1870 to 1920 and was published by Lucy Stone and her husband Henry B. Blackwell.

8   In his essay "The Significance of the Frontier in American History" (1893), Frederick Jackson Turner identified the American frontier as the place where freedom would bring out the best in the American character. As a result, old social customs and institutions would be broken down and new, more progressive and egalitarian roles would be created.

9   Correll, "Suffrage in Nebraska," 277.

10   Ibid.

11   A. Martha Vermillion, "Woman Suffrage in Thayer County," *Western Woman's Journal,* May 1881, p. 25. The Journal reported on Anthony's talk four years later in order to document the history of suffrage work in Nebraska while simultaneously providing propaganda in support of the 1880 suffrage campaign.

12   Nov. 2, 1877. Clara Bewick Colby papers, MSS M92-172. Wisconsin Historical Society (hereafter WHS), Madison, Wisconsin.

13   See, for example, the *Hebron Journal* for Feb. 20 and 27, 1879, as well as Mar. 6, 13, and 20, 1879.

14   *Hebron Journal*, Apr. 3, 1879, p. 1.

15   For analyses of the rhetorical strategies deployed by Correll and other Nebraska suffragists, see Carmen Elizabeth Heider, "Equality and Individualism: Woman Suffrage Rhetoric in Thayer County, Nebraska, 1879-1882," Ph.D. diss., Pennsylvania State University, 2000; Gaylynn Jeanne Welch, "Natural Rights Versus Moth-

erhood: A History of the Woman Suffrage Movement in Nebraska, 1871-1917," M.A. Thesis, University of Nebraska at Kearney, 1998; and Eleanor Claire Jerry, "Clara Bewick Colby and the Woman's Tribune: Strategies of a Free Lance Movement Leader," Ph.D. diss., University of Kansas, 1986.

16 *Hebron Journal*, Apr. 10, 1879, p. 4.

17 Ibid., Apr. 17, 1879, p. 4.

18 *Western Woman's Journal*, May 1881, p. 25.

19 "Women's Column," "Constitution of the Thayer County, Neb. Woman Suffrage Association, Organized on April 15, 1879." *Hebron Journal*, Jun. 12, 1879, pp. 1, 4.

20 *Hebron Journal*, May 22, 1879, p. 1.

21 Ibid., May 15, 1879, p. 1.

22 Colby, "Nebraska, Chapter XLIX." *History of Woman Suffrage*, 686.

23 The group noted, "It was decided that those being present being only a partial representation of the sentiment in our city that the officers elected should be considered as temporary, and actions of the first meeting rescinded at the second or thereafter, should it be considered desirable." Report of the First State Suffrage Association held in Omaha Nebraska, May 30th, 1880. Cook County Woman's Franchise Association Records Book. Papers of Harriet S. B. Brooks, RG 4054 AM, Nebraska State Historical Society (hereafter Brooks Papers).

24 Sheldon, *Nebraska Blue Book*, 432.

25 House Journal of the Legislature of the State of Nebraska, Sixteenth Regular Session, Begun and Held at Lincoln, January 4th, 1881 (Omaha: Henry Gibson, State Printer, 1881), 636.

26 Colby, "Nebraska, Chapter XLIX." History of Woman Suffrage, 682. The letter was dated December 4, 1880 and signed "L. R.," likely Mrs. Lucinda Russell, later active in the Nebraska WSA.

27 For a complete list of officers, see Vermillion, "Woman Suffrage in Thayer County." *Western Woman's Journal*, May 1881, p. 25.

28 Colby, "Nebraska, Chapter XLIX." *History of Woman Suffrage*, 684.

29 "Woman's Department," [Feb. 5, 1881], newspaper clipping from scrapbook, p. 13. Brooks Papers.

30 Ibid. Emphasis in original.

31 Sheldon, *Nebraska Blue Book*, 433.

32 Colby, "Nebraska, Chapter XLIX." *History of Woman Suffrage*, 686.

33 For a comprehensive list see Thomas Chalmer Coulter, A History of Woman Suffrage in Nebraska, Ph.D. diss. (Ohio State University, 1967), 23-24.

34 *Western Woman's Journal*, Sept. 1882, p. 274.

35 In spite of its early gains, Utah women were disfranchised by anti-Mormon provisions of the Edmunds-Tucker Act enacted by Congress in 1887; however, women recouped their loss when Utah was admitted as a state in 1896. As a result of pressure from the liquor lobby, Washington Territory, which gave women suffrage in 1883, disfranchised them in 1889. Wyoming was the first state to enact female suffrage when it entered the United States in 1890.

36 See Minutes, First Nebraska Woman Suffrage Convention, Erasmus M. Correll papers, MS 572, S1F3, NSHS; as well as coverage of the convention in the Omaha Republican, qtd. In Colby, *History of Woman Suffrage*, 688.

37 Minutes, First Nebraska Woman Suffrage Convention, Erasmus M. Correll papers, MS 572, S1F3, NSHS.

38 Republican, qtd. in Colby, "Nebraska, Chapter XLIX." *History of Woman Suffrage*, 688; minutes, First Nebraska Woman Suffrage Convention, Erasmus M. Correll papers, MS 572, S1F3, NSHS.

39 "Nebraska Woman Suffrage Convention." *Western Woman's Journal*, Oct. and Nov. 1881, p. 123.

40 Ibid.

41 The political fallout resulting from the Kansas campaign of 1867 and disagreements over the role of woman suffrage in the Fourteenth and Fifteenth Amendments had divided eastern woman's rights activists into two rival organizations. In 1869 Anthony and Stanton founded the National Woman Suffrage Association in New York, while in Boston, Lucy Stone and Henry Blackwell founded the American Woman Suffrage Association. See Catherine Clinton and Christine Lunardini, *The Columbia Guide to American Women in the Nineteenth Century* (New York: Columbia University Press, 2000), 123-25; Nancy Woloch, *Women and the American Experience* (New York: Alfred A Knopf, 1984) 327-37.

42 *Western Woman's Journal*, Oct. and Nov. 1881, p. 124. See also the letter from Lucy Stone to Erasmus Correll and Correll's response regarding his appointment as president of the AWSA published in the *Western Woman's Journal*, Oct. and Nov. 1881, p. 100.

43 Anthony's letter was published in the *Western Woman's Journal*, Dec. 1881, p. 141. Emphasis in origi-

nal.

44   Speakers in support of the amendment represented the AWSA, the NWSA, and the Nebraska WSA, and included Henry B. Blackwell, Helen M. Gougar, Susan B. Anthony, Margaret W. Campbell, Phoebe Couzins, Hannah Tracy Cutler, Rachel G. Foster, Elizabeth Boynton Harbert, Matilda Hindman, May Wright Sewall, and Harriette R. Shattuck, as well as a cadre of Nebraska woman suffrage supporters. See the fall 1882 issues of the *Western Woman's Journal* for details about their schedules.

45   *Western Woman's Journal*, Sept. 1882, p. 279.

46   "The American Woman Suffrage Association," *Western Woman's Journal*, Sept. 1882, p. 284.

47   *Western Woman's Journal*, Sept. 1882, pp. 282-83.

48   Ibid., pp. 285-86.

49   Coulter, 89.

50   *Omaha Herald*, Sept. 29, 1882, p. 8; qtd. in Coulter, 93.

51   *Omaha Republican*, Sept. 29, 1882, p. 8; qtd. in Coulter, 93.

52   See, for example, Aileen S. Kaditor's *The Ideas of the Woman Suffrage Movement: 1890-1920* (New York: W. W. Norton, 1981); Rebecca J. Mead's *How The Vote Was Won: Woman Suffrage in the Western United States, 1868-1914* (New York: New York University Press, 2004); Suzanne M. Marilley's W*oman Suffrage and Origins of Liberal Feminism in the United States, 1820-1920* (Cambridge: Harvard University Press, 1996); and Louise Michele Newman's *White Women's Rights: The Racial Origins of Feminism in the United States* (New York: Oxford University Press, 1999).

53   "The Nebraska Suffrage Campaign," p. 69 of Harriet Robinson Shattuck Scrapbook, Sept. – Nov. 1882 Re: Nebraska Woman Suffrage Campaign. Papers of Harriet Jane Hanson Robinson and Harriette Lucy Robinson Shattuck. Women's Studies Manuscript Collections from the Schlesinger library, Radcliffe College, Series 1, Part D, Reel 65, Series IX, Vol. 106.

54   Colby, *History of Woman Suffrage*, 691.

55   "The Nebraska Campaign," *The Woman's Journal*, Nov. 11, 1882, p. 360.

56   Colby, "Nebraska, Chapter XLIX." *History of Woman Suffrage*, 691.

57   Ibid.

58   Colby, "Nebraska, Chapter XLIX." *History of Woman Suffrage*, 692; *Official Report of the Nebraska State Canvassing Board, Election Held November 7, 1882* (Lincoln, Nebraska, n.d.), 2.

59   Ida Husted Harper, *The Life and Work of Susan B. Anthony*, Vol. II (Indianapolis: The Bowen-Merrill Co, 1898), 545, footnote 2.

60   Colby, "Nebraska, Chapter XLIX." *History of Woman Suffrage*, 690.

61   "The Women's Defeat in Nebraska," Nov. 10, 1882. Harriet Robinson Shattuck Scrapbook for Sept. – Nov. 1882, Re: Nebraska Woman Suffrage Campaign. Papers of Harriet Jane Hanson Robinson and Harriette Lucy Robinson Shattuck, Women's Studies Manuscript Collections from the Schlesinger Library, Radcliffe College, Series 1, Part D, Reel 65, Series IX, Vol. 106, pp. 70-71.

62   Addison E. Sheldon, *Nebraska: The Land and the People,* Vol. I (Chicago: The Lewis Publishing Company, 1931), 594.

63   Colby, "Nebraska, Chapter XLIX." *History of Woman Suffrage*, 692.

64   See Mrs. D.Y. King to Elizabeth Boynton Harbert, Nov. 17, 1882. Papers of Elizabeth Boynton Harbert, 5:70, The Huntington Library, San Marino, California.

65   Coulter, 107; see also the NWSA's Report of the Sixteenth Annual Washington Convention which listed receipts and disbursements for the 1882 Nebraska campaign, pp. 146, 150.

66   "Lost Her Temper," *Omaha Republican*, Nov. 9, 1882. Papers of Elizabeth Cady Stanton and Susan B. Anthony, Patricia G. Holland and Ann D. Gordon, eds. (Wilmington DE: Scholarly Resources, Inc., 1991), series 3, reel 22, frame 715.

67   "Sorry Sisters," Nov. 9, 1882, *Omaha Daily Herald*. Papers of Elizabeth Cady Stanton and Susan B. Anthony, Patricia G. Holland and Ann D. Gordon, eds. (Wilmington DE: Scholarly Resources, Inc., 1991), series 3, reel 22, frame 716.

68   Colby, "Nebraska, Chapter XLIX." History of Woman Suffrage, 692.

69   "Mrs. D. C. Brooks, An Educated and Refined Lady Departs This Life After a Long Illness," June 23, 1888, obituary from the *Omaha Herald*. Brooks Papers.

70   For information on Correll's death, see the scope and content notes for RG4430.AM: Erasmus Michael Correll Papers, NSHS; as well as his obituary published in the *Omaha World-Herald* on Sept. 6, 1895.

71   See Olympia Brown's *Democratic Ideals: A Memorial Sketch of Clara B. Colby* (n.p.: Federal Suffrage

Association, 1917).

72   See the entry for Ada M. Bittenbender in Willard and Livermore's *A Woman of the Century*. See also biographical information on Ada M.C. Bittenbender at NSHS.

73   See Sheldon, *Nebraska: The Land and the People*, 431-35; and Wilhite, 149-64.

Gaster, "Carry Nation Debates Woman Suffrage in Seward"

1   Born Carrie Amelia Moore in 1846 and married to David A. Nation in 1874, she began spelling her name "Carry A. Nation"—pun intended—when she began her anti-liquor crusade.

Hickman, "'Thou Shalt Not Vote': Anti-Suffrage in Nebraska, 1914-1920"

1   The federal amendment was ratified with the support of Nebraska's legislature and full suffrage was added to the state constitution in the same year. For a history of woman suffrage in Nebraska see Ann L. Wiegman Wilhite, "Sixty-five Years Till Victory: A History of Woman Suffrage in Nebraska," *Nebraska History* 49 (Summer 1969): 149-63, and James E. Potter, "Barkley v. Pool: Woman Suffrage and the Nebraska Referendum Law," *Nebraska History* 69 (Spring 1988): 11-18.

2   Paul Kleppner, *The Cross of Culture: A Social Analysis of Midwestern Politics 1850-1900* (New York: Free Press, 1970), 7-34; Frederick C. Luebke, *Immigrants and Politics: The Germans of Nebraska 1880-1900* (Lincoln: University of Nebraska Press, 1969), 66, 79, 87, 115; Robert Wallace Cherny, *Populist and Progressive in Nebraska: A Study of Nebraska Politics 1885-1912* (Ph.D. diss. Columbia University, 1972), 385; Luebke, *Nebraska: An Illustrated History* (Lincoln: University of Nebraska Press, 1995), 187.

3   Kleppner, *Cross of Culture*, 70; Cherny, *Populist and Progressive*, 353-57; *The Nebraska Blue Book and Historical Register*, ed. Addison E. Sheldon (Lincoln: State Journal Company, 1915), 759. Pietists and ritualists held differing views on how to attain salvation. Pietists believed it depended upon right behavior, while ritualists relied on faith. German sectarians, or splinter evangelical groups, tended to be pietistic and therefore identified with the Republican ideology, while the Reformed churches were more ritualistic.

4   Kleppner, *Cross of Culture*, 70; *Nebraska Blue Book* (1915), 759.

5   Philip Gleason, "An Immigrant Group's Interest in Progressive Era Reform: The Case of the German-American Catholics," *American Historical Review* 73 (December 1967): 372-73.

6   Luebke, *Immigrants and Politics*, 124, 128-30, 140, 182-83; Luebke, *Nebraska*, 178-80; Cherny, *Populist and Progressive*, 1; Thomas J. Jablonsky, *The Home, Heaven and Mother Party: Female Anti Suffragists in the United States, 1868-1920* (Brooklyn: Carlson Publishers Inc., 1994), 65-67.

7   Cherny, *Populist and Progressive*, 401, 403, 390; Frederick C. Luebke, "The German-American Alliance in Nebraska, 1910-1917," *Nebraska History* 49 (Summer 1968): 165. The term "German" is used somewhat loosely in these studies as it does not necessarily refer to an immigrant's point of origin, particularly prior to 1871, but to his language and culture.

8   Luebke, "The German-American Alliance," provides the best overview. See also James Clifton Child, *The German-American in Politics 1914-1917* (Madison: University of Wisconsin Press, 1939), 7, 18-19; Addison E. Sheldon, *Nebraska: The Land and the People*, vol. 1 (Chicago: The Lewis Publishing Company, 1931), 918.

9   John J. Rumbarger, *Profits, Power, and Prohibition: Alcohol Reform and the Industrializing of America, 1800-1930* (Albany: State University of New York Press, 1989), 7.

10   James C. Olson and Ronald C. Naugle, *History of Nebraska*, 3rd ed. (Lincoln: University of Nebraska Press, 1997), 215, 228-29, 274-75, 277. Prohibition most adversely affected the Democrats in 1916 when the state party split because party progressives, led by William Jennings Bryan, formed a prohibition faction against the traditional anti-prohibition party.

11   Sheldon, *Land and People*, 9, 11; *Barkley v. Pool*, testimony, 5553, Nebraska Woman Suffrage Association Papers, Nebraska State Historical Society, Lincoln, Nebraska (hereafter, Nebraska Suffrage Papers); Governor's Commission on the Status of Women, *Nebraska Women Through the Years, 1867-1967* (Lincoln: Johnson Publishing Co., 1967), 22-23; Eleanor Flexnor, *Century of Struggle: The Woman's Rights Movement in the United States* (Cambridge: Belknap Press of Harvard University Press, 1975), 307.

12   "New Woman and the Temperance Problem,"

Yearbook of the United States Brewers' Association (New York: United States Brewers' Association, 1912), 178-79.

13   "Brewery Gang Postpone Suffrage," *St. Edward* (Nebraska) *Advance*, Aug. 3, 1917, "clippings" file, Nebraska Suffrage Papers.

14   Manuela Thurner, "Better Citizens Without the Ballot: American Anti-Suffrage Women and Their Rationale During the Progressive Era," *Journal of Women's History* (Spring 1993): 33-34.

15   Ibid., 37, 33-34, 38, 44-45; Susan E. Marshall, "In Defense of Separate Spheres: Class and Status Politics in the Anti-Suffrage Movement," *Social Forces* 65 (December 1980): 311, 328, 337-38.

16   The MAOFESW was founded in May 1895 in response to suffrage victories in the 1890s. A petition with twelve signatures effectively killed a municipal suffrage bill in the state legislature that year, spurring anti-suffragists in neighboring eastern states to organize. See Marshall, "Separate Spheres," 330, and Anne M. Benjamin, *A History of the Anti-Suffrage Movement in the United States from 1895 to 1920: Women Against Equality* (Lewiston, N.Y.: The Edwin Mellon Press, 1991), 1-7.

17   Thurner, "Better Citizens," 49, 38-40; Benjamin, *Anti-Suffrage Movement*, 104.

18   *Barkley v. Pool*, testimony, 5530, Nebraska Suffrage Papers. Nebraska's suffrage leaders also went to work for the war effort, see Sheldon, *Land and People*, 922.

19   L. F. Crofoot, "Lest Catholic Men Be Misled," Nov. 2, 1914, "clippings" file, Nebraska Suffrage Papers; Thurner, "Better Citizens," 40-42, 48, 51.

20   Mary Ellen Swift, "Suffrage for Women a Handicap in Civic Work," *Woman's Protest* 3 (August 1913): 3; Thurner, "Better Citizens," 42-43; Marshall, "Separate Spheres," 336.

21   Benjamin, *Anti-Suffrage Movement*, 110-18, 112, 169-70. Theodore Roosevelt and William Jennings Bryan also traveled to Omaha during the campaign to speak in favor of woman suffrage.

22   *Barkley v. Pool*, testimony, 1244, 5530-59; "Mrs. E. P. Peck Elected Anti-Suffrage Chairman," *Omaha Bee*, Sept. 20, 1914, "clippings" file, Nebraska Suffrage Papers; Thurner, "Better Citizens," 35-36; Marshall, "Separate Spheres," 329, 331.

23   Wilhite, "Sixty-five Years Till Victory," 160; Marshall, "Separate Spheres," 331; *Barkley v. Pool*, testimony, 5535, Nebraska Suffrage Papers.

24   NMAOWS, "Nebraska Clergymen Condemn Woman Suffrage," Omaha, 1914 (New Haven: Research Publications Inc., 1977, no. 9329), 2-5, 10.

25   NMAOWS, "Manifesto," Omaha, 1914 (New Haven: Research Publications Inc., 1977, no. 9330), 6-7.

26   Crofoot, "Lest Catholic Men Be Misled."

27   "Facts Which Nebraska Women Must Face," *Omaha World-Herald*, Nov. 2, 1914, 8, "clippings" file, Nebraska Suffrage Papers. The Nebraska suffrage amendment did not automatically change the jury duty law, which specifically said "male."

28   *Barkley v. Pool*, testimony, 5551, Nebraska Suffrage Papers.

29   The National Association Opposed to Woman Suffrage peaked in 1916 with a membership of 350,000 members and twenty-five state organizations. Thurner, "Better Citizens," 30-35; Marshall, "Separate Spheres," 329-30; *Barkley v. Pool*, testimony, 5530-59, Nebraska Suffrage Papers.

30   Marshall, "Separate Spheres," 336, 339-41, 342-45; Anastasia Sims, "Beyond the Ballot: The Radical Vision of the Anti-Suffragists," *Votes for Women! The Woman Suffrage Movement in Tennessee, the South, and the Nation*, ed. M. S. Wheeler (Knoxville: The University of Tennessee Press, 1995), 105-28. Many leading members of the suffrage organizations were also involved in the "science" of race improvement. In Nebraska, NWSA president Dr. Inez Philbrick was an outspoken proponent of birth control among less desirable elements of society.

31   Benjamin, *Anti-Suffrage*, 147-51; "The Farm Woman," n.d., *Omaha World-Herald*, and "Nebraska Women Still Hopeful," unknown source, Apr. 7, 1917, "clippings" file, Nebraska Suffrage Papers. There is no proof of the rumor in the Senate Record.

32   "Senate Suffrage Bill Smothered," *Omaha Daily News*, Mar. 29, 1917; "Still Chance for Woman Suffrage," ibid.; "Germans Dupe Woman," *Hamilton* [Ohio?] *News*, July 28, 1917, "clippings" file; *Barkley v. Pool*, testimony, 5538, Nebraska Suffrage Papers.

33   Minutes of Annual Convention of Nebraska Woman Suffrage Association, Nov. 4, 1917, "writings" file, Nebraska Suffrage Papers.

34   Benjamin, *Anti-Suffrage Movement*, 180-90. See, for example, Crofoot's "Lest Catholic Men Be Misled."

35   Cherny, *Populist and Progressive*, 336.

36   Sheldon, *Land and People*, 907, 916.

37   Potter, "*Barkley v. Pool*," 12. Rosewater public-

ly debated Susan B. Anthony during Nebraska's 1882 campaign for a woman suffrage amendment; Orville D. Menard, *Political Bossism in Mid-America: Tom Dennison's Omaha 1900-1933* (New York: University Press of America, 1989), 72-75, 123-24.

38   Marshall, "Separate Spheres," 335-6; Benjamin, *Anti-Suffrage*, 54; Sims, "Beyond the Ballot," 105-28; Lois R. Noun, *Strong Minded Women: The Emergence of the Woman Suffrage Movement in Iowa* (Ames: Iowa State University Press, 1969), 50-53.

39   NAOWS, letter to the editor, *Omaha World-Herald*, Mar. 23, 1917; NAOWS, letter to the editor, *Omaha Daily Bee*, Feb. 1, 1917, "clippings" file, Nebraska Suffrage Papers.

40   Obituary of John F. Moriarty, n. d., "clippings" file, *Omaha World-Herald*, Omaha Public Library; *Barkley v. Pool*, testimony, 5541, Nebraska Suffrage Papers.

41   See for example, "The Teutonic Touch in Nebraska," *Woman's Journal*, Aug. 25, 1917, "clippings" file, Nebraska Suffrage Papers.

42   "Germans Fighting Suffrage in Nebraska," *Woman Citizen*, June 30, 1917, "clippings" file, Nebraska Suffrage Papers.

43   *Barkley v. Pool* testimony, 5534-35, Nebraska Suffrage Papers.

44   Ibid., 5547-49, 1249-50.

45   Thomas Chalder Coulter, "A History of Woman Suffrage in Nebraska, 1856-1920," (Ph.D. diss., Ohio State University, 1967), 127-34; Jane Jerome Camhi, *Women Against Women: American Anti Suffragism, 1880-1920* (Brooklyn: Carlson Publishing Inc., 1994), 108. See NMAOWS, "Nebraska Clergymen Condemn Woman Suffrage," 11, for a member list of the men's league.

46   *Barkley v. Pool* testimony, 5547, Nebraska Suffrage Papers.

47   Ibid., 5552. Stokes and Vardaman were radical feminists.

48   Benjamin, *Anti-Suffrage*, 170-90.

49   "Suffrage Referendum," Lincoln *Nebraska State Journal*, June 23, 1917.

50   "Anti-Suffragists Gather Signatures for Referendum Petition," *Omaha Daily Bee*, July 11, 1917; "263 Circulators of Anti-Petitions," *Omaha Daily News*, Feb. 15, 1918; "Antis to Renew Suffrage Fight," ibid., Apr. 22, 1917, "clippings" file, Nebraska Suffrage Papers.

51   When questioned about the extraordinary number of names in alphabetical order on the petitions, one referendum worker explained that he collected signatures up one side of the street and down the other. *Barkley v. Pool*, testimony, 4189-91, 4159-64, 4456. For a discussion of the fraud and its effects on the state's petition process see Potter's "*Barkley v. Pool*," 11-18.

Wirth, "Heckling President Wilson: Omaha Suffragist Rheta Childe Dorr"

1   Rheta Childe Dorr, *A Woman of Fifty* (New York: Funk and Wagnalls Company, 1924), 290-91, 295.

2   Dorr, 296.

3   Eileen Wirth, *From Society Page to Front Page: Nebraska Women in Journalism* (Lincoln: University of Nebraska Press, 2013), 44.

4   Wirth, 45.

5   Wirth, 45-46.

6   Dorr, 250.

7   Dorr, 288.

8   Dorr, 283.

9   Dorr, 290.

10   Dorr, 284.

11   Dorr, 291.

12   Ibid.

13   "Wilson Won't Let Women Heckle Him," *New York Times*, July 1, 1914. Syndicated reports also appeared in many other papers. See, for example, "Suffrage Issue One for States," *Richmond (VA) Times Dispatch*, July 1, 1914, or, "Woman Suffrage a State Issue," *Norwich (CT) Bulletin*, July 1, 1914.

14   Dorr, 292-93.

15   Dorr, 293.

16   Dorr, 293-94.

17   Ibid.

18   Ibid.

19   Ibid. Newspaper reports make no mention of Dorr's question about the election of US senators. (Prior to the ratification of Seventeenth Amendment in 1913, US senators were elected by state legislatures.) Instead, they quote Dorr as saying, "May I ask you a question? Is it not a fact that we have very good precedents existing for altering the electorate by the Constitution?" Wilson replied that had nothing to do with his conviction about the best way this could be done. See, "Wilson Won't Let Women Heckle Him," *New York Times*, July 1, 1914, and "Suffrage Issue One for States," *Richmond Times* Dispatch, July 1, 1914.

20 Dorr, 295.

21 Dorr, 296. The *Times* report, which was based on a White House transcript of the meeting, has Wilson complaining of cross-examination after a question by Wiley; Dorr's autobiography and other press reports attribute that part of the conversation to Dorr.

22 "Wilson Won't Let Women Heckle Him," *New York Times*, July 1, 1914.

23 Dorr, 296.

24 "Disavows Wilson Insult," *New York Times*, July 4, 1914.

25 "Heckling the President," *New York Times,* July 2, 1914.

26 "Would Be Militants," *New York Times*, July 6, 1914.

27 Dorr, 300.

28 Dorr, 299.

29 Dorr, 302.

30 Dorr, 303.

31 Dorr, 303-4.

32 Wirth, 46.

33 Wirth, 47.

Bisson-Best, "Doris Stevens: Nebraska's Forgotten Suffrage Leader"

1 Mary Trigg, *Feminism as Life's Work: Four Modern American Women through Two World Wars* (New Brunswick, NJ: Rutgers University Press, 2014), 29-30.

2 *Omaha High School Register* (Omaha, 1905), 27. omaharchives.org/archive/obooks/1905.pdf.

3 Winifred Holtby, "An Apostle of Action," *Time and Tide,* Oct. 26, 1928: 1-2.

4 Trigg, *Feminism as Life's Work*, 32.

5 Linda G. Ford, *Iron Jawed Angels, The Suffrage Militancy of the National Woman's Party, 1912-1920* (Lanham, MD: University Press of American, 1991), 29.

6 Ford, *Iron Jawed Angels*, 29.

7 "Proud of Scars of Suffrage Work," *New York Times* (hereafter, *NYT*), Jan. 7, 1911, 3.

8 "Omaha Girl Takes Degree," *Omaha World-Herald* (published as the *Morning World-Herald*, hereafter, *MOWH*), June 29, 1911, 4.

9 Winifred Holtby, "An Apostle of Action," *Time and Tide*, Oct. 26, 1928: 2-3.

10 Ford, *Iron Jawed Angels*, 69.

11 Doris Stevens, *Jailed for Freedom*, ed. Carol O'Hare (Troutdale, OR: New Sage Press, 1995), 214.

12 "Doris Stevens Will Go Abroad to Write," *Omaha World-Herald* (published as the *Evening World-Herald*, hereafter *EOWH*), Feb. 12, 1919, 8; "After The Scalp of U.S. Senator Thomas, Miss Doris Stevens of Omaha Opens Campaign in Colorado," *MOWH*, Sept. 18, 1914, 1.

13 "Woman, Charming Woman: Her Rights Eloquently Advocated by Elizabeth C. Stanton and Susan B. Anthony," *Omaha Daily Herald*, Dec. 4, 1888, 7. See also Kristin Mapel Bloomberg, "Striving For Equal Rights For All," *Nebraska History* 90 (Summer 2000): 170-94.

14 Laura McKee Hickman, "Thou Shalt Not Vote: Anti-Suffrage in Nebraska, 1914-1920," *Nebraska History* 80 (Summer 1999): 56.

15 Hickman, "Thou Shalt Not Vote," 60, 61.

16 Ibid. See also: Ann L. Wiegman Wilhite, "Sixty-Five Years Till Victory: A History of Woman Suffrage in Nebraska," *Nebraska History* 49 (Summer 1968): 149-63.

17 Barkley v. Poole, 103 Neb. 629, 173 N.W. 600 (1919). See also: James E. Potter, "*Barkley vs. Pool*: Woman Suffrage and the Nebraska Referendum Law," *Nebraska History* 69 (Spring 1988): 11-18.

18 Doris Stevens, *Jailed for Freedom* (New York: Boni and Liveright, 1920), 63.

19 Ford, *Iron Jawed Angels*, 123-24.

20 Stevens, *Jailed for Freedom* (1920), 93-94.

21 Stevens, *Jailed for Freedom* (1920), 155.

22 Stevens, *Jailed for Freedom* (1920), 186-87.

23 Stevens, *Jailed for Freedom* (1920), 190-91.

24 "Malone Weds, Sails For Europe Today," *NYT*, Dec. 10, 1921, 4.

25 Ibid.; "Miss Stevens and Mr. Malone Are To Be Married Saturday," *EOWH*, Dec. 8, 1921, 9.

26 "Dudley Field Malone's Wife Will Keep Her Own Name," *NYT*, Jan. 23, 1922, 18.

27 Linder, Douglas, Famous Trials, www.famous-trials.com/scopesmonkey/2133-biographies, copyright 1995-2018.

28 "Feminist Divorces Dudley Field Malone," *NYT*, Oct. 11, 1929. 19.

29 Ibid.

30 "Doris Stevens Says She May Study Law," *Sunday Omaha World-Herald*, Sept. 25, 1927, 1.

31 "Calls Women Victims of Inferiority Complex," *MOWH,* Sept. 28, 1927, 1.

32 Ibid.

33 "Omaha Women Assert Doris Stevens Wrong," *EOWH*, Sept. 30, 1927, 12.

34 Ibid.

35 Ibid.

36 Ibid.

37 "Miss Stevens Says Women Must Learn to Cooperate," *MOWH*, Oct. 6, 1927, 1, 3.

38 Ibid.

39 "American Feminists Parade in London," *NYT*, July 4, 1926, 4.

40 "Women Leaders Hail Miss Stevens," *NYT*, Jan. 30, 1934, 11.

41 Ibid.

42 Ibid.

43 Stevens, *Jailed for Freedom* (1995), 214.

44 Sheet Music, Doris Stevens Papers, RG3740, Series 3, Box 1, Folder 1, History Nebraska.

45 Letter from Doris Stevens to Dr. John B. White, Librarian, Nebraska State Historical Society, July 28, 1958, Donor File, History Nebraska. Doris Stevens Manuscript Record.

46 Ibid.

47 Letter from Jonathon Mitchell to Anne P. Diffendal, Manuscripts Curator, Nebraska State Historical Society, June 5, 1976. Doris Stevens Manuscript Record, History Nebraska.

48 Stevens, *Jailed for Freedom* (1995), 215.

49 Landals, Ted, "Who'll KnowWho, In or Out, of Who's Who? Class of 1905, Omaha High School, Plans First Reunion 49 Years Late," *Omaha World-Herald Sunday Magazine*, Sept. 11, 1955, 109.

50 Ibid.

51 "Omaha Born Feminist Dies," *OWH*, March 24, 1963, 30.

Potter, "Barkley vs. Pool: Woman Suffrage and the Nebraska Referendum Law"

1 A good summary of the woman suffrage movement in Nebraska is Ann L. Wilhite, "Sixty-five years Till Victory: A History of Woman Suffrage in Nebraska," *Nebraska History* 49 (Summer 1968):149-63. Also see Thomas C. Coulter, "A History of Woman Suffrage in Nebraska 1856-1920" (Ph.D. diss., Ohio State University, 1968). Many of the newspaper and other sources used in this article can be found in RG1073, Records of the Nebraska Woman Suffrage Association, State Archives, Nebraska State Historical Society.

2 The best review of the role of the German-American Alliance in Nebraska politics is Frederick C. Luebke, "The German-American Alliance in Nebraska, 1910-1917," *Nebraska History* 49 (Summer 1968): 165-85. Nebraska newspapers saw the hand of the German-American Alliance in the anti-suffrage petition drive, for example, *The Geneva Signal*, June 28, 1917, and *Nebraska State Journal*, July 24, 1917.

3 Luebke, "German-American Alliance," 179.

4 Ibid. 183; Addison E. Sheldon, *Nebraska The Land and the People*, Vol. I (Chicago and New York: The Lewis Publishing Co., 1931), 913-14. For vote totals on constitutional amendments see *The Nebraska Blue Book*, published biennially by the Clerk of the Legislature.

5 Luebke, "German-American Alliance," 177-78.

6 Wilhite, "Sixty-five Years Till Victory," 161-62; Coulter, "Woman Suffrage," 154-57; *Lincoln Star*, February 16, 1918.

7 *The Woman Citizen*, August 25, 1917; *Nebraska State Journal*, July 24, 1917.

8 Robert W. Cherny, *A Righteous Cause: The Life of William Jennings Bryan* (Boston and Toronto: Little, Brown, and Co., 1985), 190. Constitution of Nebraska, with Amendments, *The Nebraska Blue Book, 1915*.

9 *Laws of Nebraska*, 1913, 488-98.

10 *Omaha Daily News*, April 23, 1917; *Nebraska State Journal*, June 23, 1917; *Chadron Journal*, July 20, 1917.

11 As Laura McKee Hickman later demonstrated in *"'Thou Shalt Not Vote': Anti-Suffrage in Nebraska, 1914-1920,"* women were deeply involved in the leadership of the Nebraska Association Opposed to Woman Suffrage and in the larger anti-suffrage movement.

12 *Nebraska State Journal*, May 24, 1917.

13 *North Nebraska Eagle* (Dakota City), June 21, 1917.

14 *Omaha Daily News*, June 10, 1917; *Chadron Journal*, July 20, 1917; *The Woman Citizen*, August 3, 1918, February 8, 1919; Sheldon, *Land and People*, 911.

15 *Laws of Nebraska*, 1913, 491-92.

16 *Omaha World-Herald*, August 23, 1917; *Omaha Daily News*, December 5, 1917; *The Woman Citizen*, February 8, 1919. Even Secretary of State Pool began to doubt the validity of the petitions.

17 *The Woman Citizen*, February 8, 1919.

18 *The Evening State Journal*, February 14, *1918;*

Omaha Daily News, February 14, 1918. A copy of the petition in equity filed by the suffragists is in RG1073. Copies of all documents in Case File 67-127, Lancaster County District Court *(Barkley vs. Pool)* are at the Nebraska State Historical Society.

19   *The Woman Citizen,* August 3, 1918; February 8,1919.

20   Coulter, "Woman Suffrage," 166; Case File 67-127.

21   Coulter, "Woman Suffrage," 167; Case File 67-127.

22   *Omaha Daily News,* January 25-26, 1919; *The Woman Citizen,* February 8, 1919.

23   *Evening State Journal,* February 14, 1918; *The Woman Citizen,* September 15, 1917; *Omaha Daily News,* January 25, 1919.

24   *O'Neill Frontier,* January 30, 1919.

25   *Omaha Daily News,* February 14, 1918.

26   *The Woman Citizen,* August 4, 1917; February 2, 1918; February 22, 1919; *Omaha Daily News,* January 25, 1919. For a good summary of the situation regarding alien suffrage, see Hattie Plum Williams, "The Road to Citizenship: A Study of Naturalization in a Nebraska Community," Anne P. Diffendal, ed., *Nebraska History* 68 (Winter 1987): 168-82.

27   Case File 67-127; *Omaha Daily News,* January 25, 1919; *Nebraska State Journal,* January 26, 1919.

28   *Report of Cases in the Supreme Court of Nebraska,* V. 102: 799-805 (hereafter *Nebraska Reports).* Interestingly, one of the principal attorneys for the anti-suffrage group was Omahan John Lee Webster, who had successfully argued Ponca Chief Standing Bear's claim to constitutional protection in 1879.

29   Case File 67-127; *Omaha World-Herald,* March 3, 1919; *Nebraska State Journal,* January 26, 1919.

30   *Nebraska Reports* 103: 629-36; *Omaha Daily News,* March 6, 1919; *The Woman Citizen,* July 19, 1919.

31   *Nebraska Reports,* 103: 629-36.

32   Wilhite, "Sixty-five Years Till Victory," 162-63; Sheldon, *Land and People,* 961-64. A factor in the unanimous ratification of the federal amendment may have been the fact that most of the anti-suffrage, German-stock members of the legislature had been defeated in the Republican landslide of 1918.

33   *The Woman Citizen,* August 16, 1919.

34   *Nebraska State Journal,* January 16, 1919.

35   *Nebraska Senate Journal, (37th Session)* 1919, 786; *Nebraska House Journal, (37th* Session*)* 1919, 1113; *Omaha World-Herald,* March 11, 1919; *The Woman Citizen,* February 8, 1919.

36   *Laws of Nebraska,* 1919, 212-18.

37   *Laws of Nebraska,* 1969, 1017-27; *Laws of Nebraska,* 1973, LB 562.

38   For example see *Sunday Journal and Star,* September 7, 1986; *Lincoln Journal,* September 8, September 29, 1986; November 7, 1986; and *Sunday World-Herald,* October 18, 1987, 7:B. Beginning in July 1986, Nebraska newspapers, particularly the *Lincoln Journal,* the *Lincoln Star,* and the *Omaha World-Herald* have provided extensive coverage of the lottery petition controversy.